PRAISE FOR *FROM AFRICA TO 1,500 KROGER STORES*

"America and all people in the world need a pied piper. When you read this enjoyable story, you will see that we now have that pied piper. It is Manny Addo, the author of this fabulous book about a young entrepreneur's journey across the ocean and over every conceivable obstacle. The most important thing about his story is that Manny shows us how doing good for others is the secret to success for all of us: African women who need water to survive and Americans who need to come together as brothers and sisters helping each other to pursue happiness. This is the most important story in each of our lives. When you read this book, you will feel the irresistible call of this modern-day pied piper."

—Edwin J. Rigaud, chairman and owner, EnovaPremier, LLC

"This book speaks to a person's will, which is determined by a person's courage, which defies logic and tenacity, which is required to succeed."

—Stephen L. Hightower, president and CEO, Hightowers Petroleum Co.

"Manny's book is an invaluable resource for immigrants working in corporate America and aspiring to navigate the corporate ladder. It will also help hiring managers who recruit and supervise immigrants, DEI managers, and nonimmigrant associates better relate with their immigrant associates and customers."

—Joe Allen, chief diversity officer, GE Aviation

FROM AFRICA TO

1,500

Kroger

Stores

MY
AMERICAN
JOURNEY

MANNY ADDO

RIVER GROVE
BOOKS

Published by River Grove Books
Austin, TX
www.rivergrovebooks.com

Distributed by River Grove Books

Design and composition by Greenleaf Book Group
Cover design by Greenleaf Book Group

Publisher's Cataloging-in-Publication data is available.

Print ISBN: 978-1-63299-815-6

eBook ISBN: 978-1-63299-816-3

First Edition

CONTENTS

To my parents, Emmanuel Addo (for whom I was named), for instilling in me the fundamental principles of entrepreneurship, and Celestina Addo, for being the rock and glue who held our family together.

To my siblings, who took turns providing for me as their little brother when my parents were no longer able or alive to do so. Dr. Christie Agawu, thanks for allowing me to live with you and your family, a gesture that forever changed my life for the best. Esther, thank you for allowing me to move in with you as well during the very challenging stage in my life. Betty Morgan, thank you for the encouragement and companionship when the going became unbearable.

INTRODUCTION

In Ghana, we have an expression: "New York is one mile away from heaven." This expression fueled a lifelong dream of mine to come to this country. I arrived in the United States in 2001. Little did I know then that heaven would have so many problems. Nor did I know how rewarding those problems would become as I worked my way to creating my very own company.

Today, I am the CEO and founder of Natural Shea Care (NSC), which produces True Shea, an all-natural, unrefined shea butter product, as well as health and beauty products. True Shea is in fifteen hundred Kroger stores and also sold online through Amazon, Target, and Walmart. As with most startups, mine had a very humble beginning. I founded my company in my basement and started selling my products at local stores, churches, and flea markets. Today, my market is growing, and many different organizations and companies invite me to share my story with them. In 2023, I spoke at approximately fifty events, including the 2023 Growth Summit in Las Vegas, where I met with Chris Gardner, the man Will Smith played in the movie *The Pursuit of Happyness*. This speaking schedule amounts to me sharing my story almost once a week.

One time, someone asked me to speak at a weeklong business event. Not only did they ask me to speak, but they asked me to kick off this event with my story. I was honored, but why would I be the speaker to start the event?

Well, I asked, and they said, "Manny, you have a very inspirational story. This business you have started is not easy—for anyone. But you came here from Africa with so many strikes against you: no money, cultural differences, a heavy accent, the color of your skin, and so forth. And then, with all of that, you decided to fulfill your life's dream of coming to the United States. And here you are, and look what you did!"

The entrepreneurial world is really, really challenging. Most of the people coming to this business event had been beating themselves over the head, so many times, in so many ways, as they tried to get their businesses off the ground. They were hungry for inspiration. They were ready to make something happen. When I finished speaking, most of the audience walked up to me to thank me for sharing and tell me they felt my story was inspirational. I thought, *If so many people were inspired by my story, maybe I could share it with others. Maybe my story can inspire others to follow their own dreams.* So, I decided to write a book. And here we are.

I didn't write this book just because people ask me to give inspirational speeches at business events. I didn't write this book to become famous. I wrote this book for you. I wrote this book to share my story in case there is something that can help you become the person you were born to be.

If you are a small business owner who wants to grow and scale your business and place your products with major retailers, then this book is for you. If you are a corporate organization that wants to improve and grow your immigrant associates, diverse associates, African American associates, or any associates who do not fall within the norm of your corporate culture, this book is for you. If you have a business degree and want to learn how to put it to the test, this book is for you. If you want to assist companies in other countries to do business in the United States, this book is for you. If you are just starting your own business or thinking of starting your own business, this book is for you.

I did a pre-book launch event in February 2023 in Cincinnati, and there were around 150 people in the audience. I kid you not, I was on the stage for almost forty-five minutes. Afterward, about sixty people stood in line waiting to take pictures with me. One of the guys in the line said, "Manny, those children that you are talking about that used to walk four miles to fetch water in the mornings, that was me in Nigeria. That was me!" He was so excited. And I was equally excited to see how others could see themselves in my story.

While I am from Ghana, this message of realizing your own dream is universal, one that transcends continents. If you want some added inspiration and to learn how I put my own MBA to the test, keep reading. By the time you finish this book, I want you to know that, with perseverance and hard work, all dreams are possible. The American dream is real. It's waiting for you. You just have to start your journey.

The entrepreneurial journey is difficult, but the immigrant journey is also difficult and has its own challenges. I'll share some of the cultural challenges I overcame as an immigrant and how many people helped me along the way.

I was honored to have been invited to speak at the 2023 Growth Summit organized by Circana, a leading market research firm in the United States. During my presentation, I realized I was making a strong connection with a woman in the audience. She kept nodding and smiling as I talked about my early struggles as an immigrant in the United States. After my presentation, she approached me and said, "Manny, I'm not an immigrant, but my parents are immigrants. I understand exactly what you're going through."

This is a story of success. We all have the opportunity to succeed and fail. If you apply yourself, have a good product, and believe in your product, your chances of success are greater. For me, it was shea butter. What's your shea butter? It may be sitting right in front of you.

PART 1

THE DREAM

If you want to start your own business, the first question you have to ask yourself is this: "Is entrepreneurship really for me?" It's not for everybody. I don't want to discourage you, but I think I would be doing you a disservice if I didn't tell you that this journey is going to be difficult. It may not be for you. You can start something small as a side gig. You can operate it as a lifestyle business. But to get 1,500 stores and crack 10, 15, 50 million dollars, well, that kind of path is simply not for everybody.

In a way, you have to be crazy to put yourself out there, to take the risk of starting a business. One of my friends, who is also an entrepreneur, said, "Look, it's extremely difficult. You need hard work, but you also need a therapist, because you're going to go crazy." So it's not going to be easy, but if you persevere and have the right support, you can succeed.

You also have to do it for the right reasons. When I ask people why they want to start a business, they often say, "I want to be my own boss." That's the worst reason. Your own business is going to boss you more than all your bosses put together. It is a 24/7 commitment. If you want to leave your eight-to-five because your boss drives you crazy, just stay put. This entrepreneurial boss will chase you into your dreams, trust me. If you can't handle your eight-to-five boss, no way can you handle this boss. You won't be able to pay yourself, and there's no paid vacation or health insurance provided.

Growing a business is challenging and all-consuming, but it can be very rewarding. To know whether the trade-off is worth it to you, first and foremost, be honest with yourself. If it's not for you, that's okay. Keep your day job. But if it is for you . . . well, keep your day job anyway. You're going to need that experience—and money.

For me, there was no trade-off. I had a dream that could only be achieved through owning my own business. From a young age, I wanted to move to the United States and become an international businessman. Just as with a business, a dream needs a plan, so I broke my dream into four stages: First, I'd make it to the United States. Of course, that first step is no easy task. Second, I'd get an MBA. That meant I'd need to focus on my education and work experience while I was still in Ghana. Third, I'd gain experience by working for Fortune 500 companies in the United States. And fourth, I'd start my own business and use it to promote business between Africa and the United States. Seeing extreme poverty during my national service in Ghana inspired me to give back to communities that need it, and giving back is a crucial part of my upbringing.

This was my American dream. Of course, it was harder than it sounds, but with perseverance and support from the people around me, I eventually achieved all four stages of my dream. But it was a long road.

1

GOING BACKWARD
TO GO FORWARD

Being an entrepreneur runs in my blood. My father was a very successful entrepreneur, at least early in his career. He was a contractor and supplied sand and stone for the construction of Tema Harbor. He was one of the richest people in our community. He also co-founded the West Africa Secondary School in Accra New Town, a high school that is now located in Adenta.

After the completion of Tema Harbor, the supply contract came to an end. My father invested his entire fortune in building a salt manufacturing factory, but he failed miserably. He went into road construction before salt and continued with road construction when the salt business failed. He switched from distribution to manufacturing, a skill set he did not have. This mistake taught me that manufacturing and distribution require two different skill sets, a lesson I have carried with me to today and that has guided my business decisions. I learned at a very early age that it is better to do what you excel at. My father never quite recovered, but he also never gave up.

My birth coincided with my father's business downfall. Due to the timing of my birth, I had a relatively hard time in relation to my siblings; I grew up struggling a lot. My father taught me to always go the extra mile—a lesson that has helped me throughout my life. It might not always lead to success, but it is always worth the effort.

I am the youngest of eight siblings. There is a big gap in our ages, with the oldest being almost twenty years older than me. Some of my older siblings were old enough to be my parents. And sometimes when they took me out, some people thought they were my parents. We had a unified and very harmonious and respectful family. My parents rarely argued in front of us. We all got along. We all had a deep faith in God and went to church a lot.

While my father was the breadwinner, my mother was the pillar of the home. She organized and ran the house, providing stability and peace. Everyone in our home, including my father, depended on my mother. She was a very devoted Christian and the women's leader for the Greater Accra Region for the Ghana Apostolic Church. I went with her to the women's meetings and conventions. My role was to record the service and testimonials on a tape recorder. Most of the time, I would be the only male in these meetings, which gives you an idea of how close we were.

When my father's business started declining, my mother began selling belongings she had acquired over the years during my dad's successful days. She hustled to take care of our household, including providing food, covering my room and board and school fees, and paying the water and electricity bills. Her perseverance served as a buffer from the economic hardships at home.

When I was fifteen, my mother was in a car accident on her way to Somanya to pay her condolences to the family of the chairman of the Ghana Apostolic Church. She ended up paralyzed from a spinal cord dislocation. During her stay in the hospital, the family took turns visiting and taking care of her, waking up every morning at 5:00 and sometimes even visiting her in the evening to pray for her. My sister Esther, who is six years older than me, pretty much moved into the hospital to look after our mom. Mom's hospitalization coincided with my summer vacation that year, and I used to visit her a few times a week, although the distance from my home to the hospital was about thirty miles. It took me five hours each day to make the journey.

Because of her leadership position in the church, the whole congregation was praying for her. But even with all these prayers, she died after six months. I was devastated. My mother, my best friend and mentor, was taken away from me. Her death challenged my faith in Christ quite a bit. I wanted to know why God took my mother away.

This was the beginning of things falling apart for the family, but especially for me. As the youngest, I had relied heavily on the support of my mother. Without her, I was searching for something to hold on to. There was a huge vacuum in my life that led to a lot of struggle. But I told myself that, no matter what the circumstances were, I needed to get out of this situation. I needed to follow my mother's example—in faith and perseverance. I later on said to myself that maybe God was just preparing me for the struggle I would encounter when I came to the United States. Sometimes you have to go backward to go forward.

Without my mother's constant hustle, our family began to struggle financially. My school fees were late, and the utility companies started turning off our water and electricity. More than once, our utilities were turned off during the Christmas holidays because we were behind on our bills. We sometimes spent Christmas in the dark. Worst of all, we sometimes went without food during the holidays. Clothing or gifts were a luxury I couldn't even imagine at the time. This experience left a bitter taste in my mouth about the holidays, which lingers to today.

Eventually, I embraced what I had learned from both my parents: my father's entrepreneurship and my mother's perseverance and hustle. I started looking for ways to bring in extra income to help support the family. I started selling products as a middleman. This was the beginning of my own hustle. I carried on arranging sales from high school all the way through college, where I used to distribute clothes from retailers in Tema to the University of Cape Coast, where I was enrolled.

FAMILY SUPPORT

Education is an equalizer. When I look around, most people who have done well have done it through education. I always did my best to keep my grades up in school and keep advancing. That is what really saved me. Had it not been for school, I would have taken a different path. The way out for me was through education. In Ghana, preparatory school is first grade through sixth grade. Each student has to take an exam at the end. This exam is taken on the same day in five countries. A student's fate after six years is determined in four hours. The results determine what secondary school you go to, and the secondary school you go to is extremely important to who you become.

I owe a lot of who I am today to my late brother Jake, who was sixteen years older than me. When I was in sixth grade, the year of the big final exam, I hated him like crazy. He would wake me up every morning at 5:00 and he would tutor me in math and science and make me do my homework before leaving for school. I didn't enjoy it back then, but by the time I took my final exam, I was on top of my game. Because of Jake's help, I was admitted into one of the best schools in the country, Achimota School.

Of course now, I appreciate what he did for me. This struggle prepared me for my next success by showing me the importance of hard work. That's where perseverance comes from: from that grit, that determination, that hardship.

Most of my siblings took turns one way or the other in raising me, because I was the youngest. From a broader perspective, this is a reflection of African culture. Out of generosity, people do that—everywhere, not just in my house. It's an unspoken rule: If you do well, you help others. You help because it's the right thing to do, but it also serves as a type of community insurance. You have family insurance and friend insurance to help you through the rough times, and like insurance, you must pay into it when you can. Today, I still help my family in Ghana from time to time. I send them money and support them however I can to pay back what they gave me when I was in need during my formative years.

When I attended Achimota School, I lived in a boardinghouse for five years, and this is where I formed lifelong friendships. My mother passed in my third year, and I began struggling. I lost focus. My grades went down. I started smoking and drinking, and got into all kinds of trouble. I literally lost my way.

At the end of the fifth year in secondary school, students are required to take an external exam called the Ordinary Level. I failed this exam and was not able to continue my education to what we called sixth form. I had to retake the exam.

At this point, my sister Esther had become almost like a second mother to me. She asked me to move in with her while I was preparing to retake my Ordinary Level exam. Her home provided me with the stability I needed to focus on studying. I passed with flying colors and proceeded to the sixth form.

During this period, my father was not always in a position to provide for the family, so the rest of us, especially my brother Jake, stepped up. I began helping, too, selling products here and there to make ends meet. I would find friends and family who were in retail and had goods and would connect them—for a commission—with individuals who needed these products. Very soon, I became a mini broker in my community. I sold shoes, shirts, watches, biscuits, cars, China-made jeans, and women's clothing. I continued this work all the way through college. My room was a mini retail store; I sold clothes to students and distributed biscuits and canned products to the stores in Cape Coast.

My sister Christie introduced me to one of her friends, who was the general manager of one of the first privately owned TV stations in Ghana. He gave me a job as a commissioned salesman. Some of you might know that commissioned sales is one of the most difficult jobs around. My job was to get businesses to buy ads at the station. Now I had upgraded my hustle to a more formal role, and this gave me a full-blown experience in the corporate business environment.

NATIONAL SERVICE

In Ghana, education is subsidized by the government. So when you're done with either high school or college, you have to do what we call national service, to serve your nation for the education you received. It lasts for one year. In my time, national service was before college, so when I was done with high school, I was placed as a school teacher in the most remote village in Ghana, if not the most remote village in the world. This village is called Tansia.

Now, when I say remote, I mean it's a dead end. To give you some perspective, let me say this: There's poor, and there's Africa poor. They are two different things. In the village of Tansia, there was no plumbing, no good roads, and no electricity. To get drinking water, you'd have to walk four miles in the morning and return with a bucket of water on your head. Though we struggled at home in Tema sometimes to pay the bills, at least we had access to water and electricity. Tansia was a new life—a proper cultural shock.

There was no transportation to the village either. Twice a week, a semitruck towing a wooden structure came to the village. To get to the next village, you'd have to sit in this wooden cart with goats and sheep, not just other people. If you weren't careful, you might be hit with a horn of a cow. If you had to do anything in the nearest towns, it had to be on Tuesdays and Thursdays, which were market days, or you'd have to ride a bike or walk for twenty miles.

We lived in a compound—a big house with smaller mud houses surrounding it, forming a circle. Each house contained five or six different families, and there was a common area in the center. This communal space was where people congregated in the evening, having conversations, drumming, dancing, drinking, and having fun. All the families were there—men and women, boys and girls, all lying in the open area. The mud houses were built like a fort, with one very small window. The houses were designed for protection rather than comfort, to keep the people safe from wild animal attacks.

During the day in the northern part of Ghana, where Tansia is, the temperature runs from about 80 to 140 degrees. At that temperature, it's almost unbearable to even live or sleep in the house during the day. If you wanted to take a nap, you had to find a shady area under a tree. It was too hot to sleep in the huts, which averaged more than 100 degrees. But sleeping outside meant you had to deal with all the flies. In the evening, we'd all begin the night by sleeping outside, because it was too hot inside. When we couldn't take the bug bites any longer, we'd move into our room. This was a very uncomfortable way for anyone to live. Between the poverty and the mosquitos, many people in Tansia died of malaria, an ailment that can be cured with twenty dollars' worth of medication.

While I was in Tansia , I taught social studies, cultural studies, history, and English. The poverty extended to the school, of course. There was no furniture. We sat on hard wooden slabs with cement blocks serving as legs. We had some books and some pens and paper—very limited supplies. Two or three people shared the same book. The students wrote notes on the palms of their hands. The school didn't have a roof, so when it rained, we all had to go home.

The people of Tansia are very hardworking, and they embraced me and my colleagues from the south who were there teaching. They were extremely happy to have us in the village and did their best to make us comfortable. Most days, they would fetch water for us so we didn't have to do the four-mile walk. They often brought us food and drinks.

Tansia was famous for a local drink called *pito*, which locals drank on a daily basis. Pito is a locally brewed alcohol; it becomes more bitter as its alcohol content increases by the day. They swore by two things: pito and shea butter. Pito cured most internal ailments, and shea butter cured all external ailments. I got so accustomed to pito that I continued to drink it when I returned to Tema after my national service ended. When I visited the Northern Region again in 2023, after thirty years, the first thing I asked for was pito.

One of the good things about Tansia and its region is that there is plenty of shea butter. Shea trees primarily grow in the wild northern part of Ghana. Locals use shea butter for everything: They cook with it. They use it for their hair and their skin. I tried cooking with shea butter out of curiosity and necessity. I was curious to see how it would taste, and it was cheaper than the other oils on the market. Since I was not used to it, it didn't taste as good as what I was used to, but it did the job.

I got to know the people of Tansia really well, and their situation affected me more than it would have if I'd only seen it on television. By spending time with them, I know how smart they are, but I know how tired they are as well. The kids usually came to school late, and I'd ask why. They'd say they had to fetch water with their mother or help on the market day. This was a reason I fully understood. I wished I could have helped these kids because I knew how hard they worked. But there were no opportunities to transform this hard work into success.

If there is no opportunity, no amount of hard work and intelligence can save you. If they had been born anywhere else—from the south of Ghana to anywhere in the United States—it would have been different. These children could be president of Ghana or the CEO of a major company, but they simply don't have that opportunity. But even without much hope, the people of Tansia keep moving forward, trying to build a better life. They persevere.

After I completed national service, I returned to Tema, in the south. But I made a mental promise to myself that if I ever got out of Ghana and made my way to the United States, I would do my best to bring economic development to places like Tansia.

KEEP ON MOVING

After national service, I went to college at the University of Cape Coast, and I graduated with a four-year degree in social science (sociology and economics, with a minor in education). During this period, my older siblings and I continued to supplement my father's efforts in taking care of the family. We all pulled together to keep the family afloat, facing whatever challenges arose.

My big brother, who was affectionately called F'Atta or F'Ta for short, had taken over the mantle of family provider from Jake at this point. F'Ta took care of me through the first few years of college, until he got sick. Eventually, his diabetes affected his kidneys and his legs, and he was longer able to walk on his own. This condition led to the deterioration of his sand and stone business, and he was no longer able to provide for me. As his illness escalated, other siblings and I took turns taking care of him. While I was on holidays, I helped him to the bathroom, to doctors' appointments, to church services, and even to see a traditional priest. Although we were Christians, at one point, we were so desperate that we were willing to try anything and everything.

He was admitted to Korle-Bu Teaching Hospital in his final days. This was the same hospital where my mother had been admitted many years earlier. I again had to make the five-hour journey to visit him. At this point, I was much older and was able to play a lead role in his care. I guess visiting my mother years earlier had prepared me for this job. The most difficult times were when I had to carry him on my back up a flight of stairs to take him from one floor to another for X-rays because the elevators were not working. He died not too long after his kidneys failed, so we were not able to get him a transplant or dialysis.

The death of my brother coincided with my sister Christie, who had earned a PhD in sociology, relocating with her family back to Ghana from the United States. I was still in college at the time, and when she saw the conditions I was living in at home, she asked me to live with her. So I stayed with Christie for the rest of my schooling. She provided a stable home environment and the financial support that enabled me to graduate from college. She became my mother figure while I was studying. Today, she lives in New Jersey and is my partner in leading our shea butter efforts in Ghana.

After college, I worked for Maersk from 1999 to 2001. Maersk is a global 2000 company, one of the largest shipping companies in the world. I worked as a logistics officer and was responsible for nontraditional exports, including bananas and pineapples, to various countries around the world. As a logistics officer, I was involved in preparing bills of lading, customs clearance procedures, and the transportation of products. This supply chain experience would come in handy later on. I still use Maersk to ship my products, and some of my colleagues and friends from twenty years ago still work with the company.

Through all of the struggle, losses, and hardships, I learned the crucial lesson of perseverance. No matter what comes, whether that's a family illness or a failing business, you have to just keep moving forward. You have to hustle. You have to persevere. This lesson is fundamental for starting your own business. But you can never persevere alone; you need the support of your family, your community, your mentors and cheerleaders.

2

STRUGGLES AND SUPPORT

With my degree in hand, it was time to make my American dream come true, but to do that, I needed to get to America. I applied to several U.S. MBA programs, but in the meantime, I tried to get a short-term visa to visit my family in New York and New Jersey. I discovered that getting a visa to the United States when you're coming from a developing country is extremely difficult. Very few people receive a visa, but even to apply requires traveling to the American embassy for an interview. In order to get to the interview, I had to leave home at 3:00 a.m. or sleep at a friend's place in Accra, where the embassy is located, to arrive on time.

This process is so competitive that the people who live close to the embassy have turned their easy access into a business. Because they live close by, they can get to the embassy before anyone coming in from out of town. They fill all the seats in an area outside the building at 3:00 a.m., and then, when applicants begin arriving around 6:00

or 7:00 a.m., the locals start selling the seats to them. The later the applicants arrive, the more they have to pay just to wait for a visa and an interview. Most of us are turned down for a visa anyway.

Over a span of six years, I was rejected for a U.S. visa twice. The first time, I was in my second year of college. The second time was about four years later. I went to the embassy to try my luck for a third time. This time, at two o'clock in the afternoon, I heard my name called. I approached the counter with prayers. I was nervous and happy at the same time. When I reached the counter, the lady said, "You have a five-year, multiple-entry visa to the United States." I guess the third time really is the charm. This visa allowed me to visit the United States as many times as I wanted within five years.

I was elated. I couldn't believe I finally had my visa! It was one of the happiest days of my life. When I went home that evening, my friends and I celebrated. As we say in Ghana, New York is one mile away from heaven.

It took me a while to save to buy a ticket, but when I had enough money, I took a month's vacation from my job at Maersk to visit my sister and her family in Princeton, New Jersey, and my niece and nephew in the Bronx. I planned to enjoy the long vacation.

In Ghana, we grew up thinking that in the United States, the roads are paved in gold. All the movies we saw were from Hollywood. As far as we were concerned, once someone arrived in the United States, sooner or later, they would become rich.

I was about to receive a big dose of reality.

VICE VERSA

During my limited one-month visit to the United States, I faced a major crossroads in my life. I got accepted into the MBA program at Xavier University in Cincinnati, Ohio. But I was in the States on a tourist visa that would not allow me to work or go to school. In order to attend Xavier, I'd need a student visa.

The most appropriate thing to do was to go back to Ghana, resign from my job at Maersk, apply for a student visa, and prepare to come back to Xavier University. Sometimes you have to go backward to go forward, right? However, this logical option had many potential problems. First, I already knew that getting a visa to the United States was very challenging, and there was a possibility that I might not even get a student visa if I went back to Ghana. Second, I'd have to buy another plane ticket, which was very expensive. Given my financial circumstances, that would be difficult.

The second option was to resign from my job while remaining in the United States, inform my friends and family of my decision not to go back, and proceed to Xavier University with the hope of converting my visitor's visa to a student visa.

I looked at this situation from an entrepreneurial perspective. I considered the following factors:

- I was already in the United States, so why go back?
- I might not be able to return to the United States after I left.
- Returning was also going to be expensive because I had to get a new ticket.
- I had enough information to take a calculated risk.
- I had gained admission to attend Xavier University, and I could lose my position there if I was delayed in returning to the United States.

Although both situations posed a visa challenge, going to Xavier and converting my visitor's visa to a student visa was more probable than going back to Ghana to apply for a student visa from abroad.

With this analysis, I decided to stay in the United States and proceed to Cincinnati to start my MBA. I sent a letter of resignation to Maersk and informed my friends and family about this new development. This was the first spontaneous decision I had ever made, and it would shape the rest of my life and my career. I didn't realize it yet, but this was the first time I had seized a crucial chance and run with it. I would have to make several more spontaneous decisions like this in my career. Some of them I miscalculated badly, but most of them have benefited me greatly. Don't be afraid to embrace opportunity!

The support of my family and community had been crucial to getting me to this point. Since I wasn't going back, it was time to share the few belongings I had accumulated over the previous year and a half working with Maersk. I gave my clothes to my brother Jake; without him, none of this would have been possible. I gave my television and fridge to my other siblings. And that was that. Without returning home, I had moved to the United States. As much as my family wanted to see me back, they knew I'd been longing for this journey for twenty years. The first step of my American dream was complete. I had made it to the United States!

Unfortunately, this was the summer of 2001, and September 11 was about to change everything.

THE STRUGGLE HAD JUST BEGUN

My sister Christie gave me one thousand dollars, and after paying the bus fare and other expenses, I had six hundred dollars when I arrived in Cincinnati at 3:00 a.m. I checked into the university's recommended hotel, paying seventy dollars a night. At this rate, I would burn through my money rather quickly and might be homeless sooner rather than later. I also hadn't paid my tuition yet. I'd need forty to fifty thousand dollars to get through the first year.

With this realization, I spoke to the receptionist the next day. "I just got admitted to Xavier University," I said, "and I can't afford seventy dollars a night." Fortunately for me, the receptionist was a student at Xavier, and he agreed to help me find another place to stay. He took me around town, and we found an apartment. First thing Monday morning, he helped me move into my first apartment, which I shared with four other people. All I had was a suitcase and a blanket my sister had given me.

I slept on that blanket on the floor. I didn't have a pillow. I didn't have a chair or a table. I wondered how I'd study for my MBA without a chair and table. My roommates felt sorry for me, and they must have told their parents there was an African kid who was struggling in the building. Whenever they came back from visits home, they would bring me a pillow or a jacket from their mothers. One gave me a microwave, and another gave me a television. Gradually, I started acquiring possessions in that room, and it began to feel like a home. I hadn't expected to find the same sort of community insurance I'd had back home, but there it was, and I was very grateful for it.

As I settled in, I prepared my application for a student visa. My sister had agreed to cosign for a student loan to pay for my fees and lodging, but I wouldn't be eligible for the loan until the visa came through. I applied for the visa the last week of August 2001. Typically, this was a pretty straightforward six-week process. But then 9/11 happened. There were a lot of unknowns and confusion after the attacks, including around the visas the hijackers were using to enter the U.S., leading to scrutiny of the visa conversion program. For me, that meant a six-week process became a nine-month one.

I couldn't get a loan without that visa, and I couldn't work either. This led me to fall behind on my school fees, rent, books, food—everything. After my first month's rent—$225, I remember vividly—I was dead broke. When it came time for the second month's rent, my six hundred dollars were long gone. I began leaving the house every morning at 7:00, because I knew my landlord would come at 8:00 a.m. to ask for his rent. I would go to school and not return until 1:00 a.m. the next day. Xavier was running out of patience for their school fees as well, and I could no longer go to the cafeteria because I'd run up a tab with them too. I couldn't even use a vending machine, as that was my first time seeing one and I had no idea how it worked. At this point, I discovered a Chinese restaurant with a lunch buffet for $4.25. That was the first buffet I'd ever seen. All you can eat—wow! I began eating there six or seven times a week.

Fortunately, being out of the house with no job and no money to do anything meant that I had plenty of time to study. I spent a lot of time in the library, but the academic workload was way more than I had anticipated. This was compounded by the fact that I didn't have furniture in my room and did not own a computer, which almost all the other students had, so it was difficult to study at home. My computer literacy skills were very limited, while most of the other students had grown up with them, and they were already working with Fortune 500 companies. I felt very far behind.

UNIFORM CONNECTIONS

One semester, a professor asked us to interview a leader and write about them for a course. Not only did I see this as a chance to catch up with my classmates, but I immediately put on my entrepreneur's hat and saw beyond the school project. I asked myself, "Which leader in Cincinnati can I interview that might lead to a business opportunity later down the road?" I looked around and identified a company named Cintas Corporation. They are a Fortune 500 company that distributes uniforms.

I chose Cintas because the uniform manufacturing industry is labor intensive, and my research had shown that they were sourcing from places like China and Mexico. I saw that it made economic sense to source the uniforms from Ghana instead because of its relatively cheaper wage rate than China. In order to produce uniforms in Ghana, manufacturers would have to source the materials and machines from China and ship them to Ghana. This was an added cost. However, certain economic tariffs helped to make this process workable. Ghana waives the import tariffs for manufacturing inputs for products to be exported. The U.S. African Growth and Opportunity Act (AGOA) is a preferential trade program that allows countries in sub-Saharan Africa to export products to the United States tariff-free. The combination of these trade preference policies with cheaper wages in Ghana would enable the production of uniforms in Ghana to be competitive with China.

Armed with this analysis, I went in search of the CEO of Cintas Corporation. I sent a few emails and a letter but did not get a response. One day in a class, we were divided into small groups for discussion. One of the ladies in my group introduced herself as a manager at Cintas Corporation. I introduced myself and asked her if she could get me an interview with the CEO for my leadership project. She promised to do her best, and less than a week later, I got an email from the CEO's executive assistant saying that I had an interview with the CEO, Scott Farmer.

I bought my first suit at age thirty-three and wore it to the interview. For the first twenty-five minutes of the thirty-minute interview, I asked Mr. Farmer about the qualities of a good leader, the challenges and how he copes with them, his work-life balance, and his family. But I saved the best for last. During the last five minutes, I presented the opportunity to source uniforms from Ghana for Cintas Corporation and shared how this was possible based on cheaper labor, AGOA, and the free zones designation. I also demonstrated my knowledge about Cintas Corporation, sharing their sales revenues and their cost of operation and manufacturing. I had almost memorized the Cintas annual report! I showed him how much sourcing from Ghana could improve their bottom line.

At the end of our talk, Mr. Farmer gave me a copy of the Cintas handbook, which I still refer to from time to time. He walked me all the way from his office down the stairs to the reception on the ground floor, a gesture that has stuck with me to this day. It was a very humble gesture for the most important person I had ever met—the CEO of a Fortune 500 company whose family owns the company.

I soon received an email from Brian Bensman, who introduced himself as the senior director of supply chain at Cintas. He said Mr. Farmer had shared my opportunity with him, and he invited me for a meeting. I showed up alone, only to find out this meeting was a very serious meeting, with about six other Cintas associates, including his boss, Kevin Bien. They asked me the name of my company, but I told them I didn't have one. I was just a student at Xavier University. However, I was extremely prepared for the meeting and was able to convince them of the opportunity. They brought me on as a vendor and ended up sending me to Ghana to inspect factories to manufacture their uniforms.

While in Ghana on this trip I met with Vice President John Dramani Mahama, who later became the president of Ghana. I shared the Cintas opportunity with him. He introduced me to the CEO of Agricultural Development Bank for funding. During this trip I also met with the CEO of Ghana Export-Import Bank, Dr. Abdul-Nashiru Issahaku, who later became governor of the Bank of Ghana. Dr. Issahaku, a true believer in exporting products from Ghana, helped me get a grant to export products to the United States.

The Cintas Diversity Supply Program really helped me in this process. I credit Cintas Corporation with my supply chain expertise and experience, for believing in me and providing me the opportunity to prove myself. To this day, Scott Farmer continues to be my mentor.

However, I did not personally meet him again until almost twenty years after that first meeting. I finally met him again in the Cintas Suite at an FC Cincinnati game (Farmer is one of the owners of the team).

He continued his mentorship by introducing me to the Farmer School of Business at Miami University to share my entrepreneurial journey and also to Orchid Holdings, an investment firm his family is associated with.

Scott Farmer and Cintas were instrumental in helping me start my journey to fulfilling my entire American dream. By connecting Cintas with a manufacturer in Ghana, I began my mission of promoting business between Africa and the United States. It was all coming together, a piece at a time.

WITH A LITTLE HELP FROM MY FRIENDS

Because of my coursework, I had to work at night. My first job was working at a warehouse. I would go to class from 6:00 p.m. to 9:00 p.m., catch a bus to get to my warehouse job before 10:00 p.m., then return home around 6:00 or 7:00 a.m. I'd take a short rest and then study before I went to class. All the struggles piled on at once, but I did what I had to do to make money and get good grades.

With all the social challenges, economic challenges, and academic challenges, things began to fall apart. So, I did what I would have done at home: I reached out to my community, the few friends and family I knew in the United States. My sister gave me another seventeen hundred dollars for fees, and my friends would send me fifty or one hundred dollars from time to time. I would not have survived without their support.

Africans have a different sense of time than Americans. When I arrived in the United States, I made it a point to turn over a new leaf by being on time to my classes so I would get the best out of being in school. The first day, I initially arrived about five minutes late, which was an improvement over me being regularly thirty minutes late in Ghana. To my surprise, the class was already in full session. The next day, I decided to come exactly on time, and—again to my surprise—everybody was already seated, and I was the last person to walk in. The third day, I decided to arrive a few minutes before class began. About 90 percent of the students were there, seated, and waiting for the professor. I began to realize the importance of time in my new country.

Then came Thanksgiving. I didn't know what Thanksgiving was, but discovered it was a day without school. At lunch on Thanksgiving day, I went to my beloved Chinese restaurant, but the door was locked. A sign in the window said, "Closed for Thanksgiving." I was so confused. *What on earth is Thanksgiving?* I wondered.

I walked home very disappointed, wondering where my next meal would come from. A few minutes later, I heard a knock on my door. It was my next-door neighbor. She had a plate of food in her hands and said that her daughter saw me trying to get into the Chinese restaurant. She brought me my first Thanksgiving meal. It was a godsend.

This woman's kindness made me feel at home. In the United States, people are often in their own world, taking care of their own families but paying no attention to their neighbors. They are, as you may hear, "minding their own business." In Ghana, you are your neighbor's keeper. We look after one another. Your neighbor provides food if you are hungry, and you do the same for them. Americans might interpret this as meddlesome or nosey, but in Ghana, it's how we care for one another.

As a classic example, during one visit to Ghana, I went to my lawyer's office. He was looking out his window and saw two men arguing, getting ready to fight. Instead of closing the window to block the noise, my attorney stepped out onto his balcony and yelled, "Hey, guys! Stop. Just stop." And they stopped fighting. As a community leader, my attorney is able to do that because, when those guys need help, they go to him, and he provides money or advice. They respect him.

In Ghana, if you have young children and need to go somewhere, such as to the market or to work, there's no need to hire a babysitter. You can just leave your kids with your neighbor. They likely are more than happy to help take care of your children; it is both accepted and expected. And when the time comes, you're happy to take care of their children too. Your neighbors will also defend your children, if necessary, from abuse or threats. You don't even have to be there. But in that same vein, your neighbors are allowed to discipline your child for you. It goes back and forth; while in their care, the neighbor treats your child like their own. Ghana is a "we" society: It's not just me and you but a community. We take care of one another.

I met another guardian angel, Jennifer Bush, on campus. She was and is still the assistant dean at Xavier's business school. She gave me all kinds of teaching and graduate assistantship opportunities so I could get a little bit of money to cover tuition costs. She was one of my first mentors in the United States, and I could not have graduated without her help. Without her, my story would have taken a very different turn.

Jennifer introduced me to the Bellarmine Chapel, the center of Catholic ministry at the university. That's where I met Father Bollman, the Catholic priest at Xavier University. One day, I was so overwhelmed I didn't know what else to do, so I visited Father Bollman. I was crying on my knees, telling him my problems. I told him I was dead broke and needed a loan in order to continue my education. He was touched and told me to follow him. I had no idea what he had in mind.

He took me to the administration building. He wanted to check my grades to make sure I was a serious student before he lent me some money. He was impressed that I had received all As. Of course I had all As! I was in the library eighteen hours a day, hiding from my landlord! He was so impressed that he gave me a five thousand dollar loan for food, rent, books, and so on. His generous gesture saved my life at the time, and we are good friends to this day.

In order to show my appreciation, I would help Father Bollman clean the church. One Christmas Day, I approached Father Bollman after Mass to help clean up and take down the lights and decorations. It was about 9:00 p.m. when we started and around 10:30 p.m. when we finished. It was 5 degrees outside, and being from Africa, I wasn't used to the cold, so I was shivering as I carried a heavy ladder to help get the lights down. Father Bollman followed me to the basement as I put the ladder away. He said, "Manny, I don't want to see you here anymore. Go study. I appreciate it, but you don't need to help me anymore."

During the Christmas break, all my roommates went home, and I was left alone. The library, my safe haven, was closed over the break as well. I kept remembering the saying "This too shall pass." So, instead of worrying or feeling lonely, I asked myself, "How can I make the best out of this situation?" And the answer I got was "get good grades."

I had no other option but to spend my time with my books, so I buckled down. I decided to test out of Marketing 801, and I passed the test and saved myself about a thousand dollars in tuition. I ended up getting my MBA in marketing in eighteen months. With my MBA, the second stage of my American dream was now complete!

3

CULTURE SHOCK

On one of my first days in New York, I had my first taste of culture shock. During my stay in New York, I lived with my nephew and niece. One day on my way back home after visiting the city, I passed a few White men sitting under a tree. They were wearing casual clothes, drinking beer, and smoking, and they seemed to be enjoying the shade. They had a couple of dogs with them that seemed to be well behaved. As I walked past, one of the men asked me for a quarter.

Now, at this point, I was a little confused. When I got home, I yelled to my cousins, "Guys, come listen! Can you believe this? Some White guy under a tree asked me for a quarter!"

They burst out laughing, and I asked them why. They said, "Manny, they're homeless people." I had finally made it to "one mile away from heaven," and apparently there were people begging on the street. But this wasn't the poverty I'd seen back home. This man was wearing gym shoes and jeans. He was drinking a can of beer. And he had a dog that looked happy and healthy. Why would this man be asking me for money?

I found it hard to wrap my head around someone being homeless in this land of opportunity, with so much abundance all around. Adding to my confusion was that I'd never seen a homeless person who could afford a can of beer or care for an animal. And it was a White person!

Now, there wasn't anything unusual about this homeless person. He was just going about his day. The unusual piece was *me*. As a foreigner, an outsider, I interpreted the situation differently from how a native New Yorker—or even my niece and nephew, who'd been there four or five years at that point—would. In order to build a successful business in this country, grow your professional expertise, serve as a consultant, or help companies do business with a foreign economy, it's important to learn the culture and the economy of the other country. It's important to notice and embrace these moments of culture shock and maybe even use them.

For example, there is a stereotype that Africans are aggressive. Sometimes we show up without calling and barge in. In Ghana, sometimes five or more people are sleeping in a room, and there is no space for privacy. One more person doesn't make much difference. You just pop in and visit someone. They drop everything and spend time with you. If you just show up, it shows the strength of your friendship.

Here, that would be culturally wrong. People in the United States value their space and distance a lot, even from their friends. Typically, you let them know if you are going to visit. If you are going to talk to someone, you schedule a call; you don't just walk into their office. And you ask before you take their food, or you might get bitten. Africans are not aggressive; we just don't know these rules. It is not better or worse; it's just different.

In Africa, we sometimes eat from the same bowl, often without asking. That's not because there aren't enough bowls or because we want to steal one another's food; it's because we are friends. We trust one another to share our space, our food, and our time. We have that closeness. But when you bring that to the United States, it translates very differently.

When I was working at PNC Bank, I walked into the kitchen and a good friend of mine was eating chicken wings. I thought I'd like to have a chicken wing, and I reached in and took one. He was so upset he almost chopped off my hands. I thought we were friends, which meant we could share with each other; he also thought we were friends and I should respect his boundaries. This is where our different cultures collided. We eventually came to understand each other's differences, but it took time and a willingness to learn. Now I know the rule: Don't take someone's food here unless they offer it to you. Sometimes immigrants import their behavior to the United States, which obviously creates cultural problems.

These things translate into how we interact with others. America is the great melting pot—a bubbling mixture of different cultures. And every culture—especially your own—brings something unique to the table. I have tried to use the best of my two cultures to create opportunities for connection, learning, and business growth. These differences have shaped my life. Understanding them allows me to look at things from another perspective. There are other ways of doing things than what I am accustomed to. Allowing myself to embrace the differences between the cultures is why I am thriving here.

A FIRM HANDSHAKE

On my graduation day from the MBA program, two of my favorite people, Father Bollman and Jennifer Bush, came to congratulate me. It made me so happy. And it made them so happy too. I was their success story. They were my family. The small community I had built helped me through some rough times.

After graduation, I went to say thank you to Father Bollman for all he had done for me while I was in school. After we finished our conversation, he shook my hand and said congratulations. I responded with a very weak handshake. So, when I turned around to leave, he called me back.

He said, "Manny, you are getting ready to go into the workforce. You have to give people a firm handshake." This was a good learning moment for me: in the United States, a strong handshake is preferred. Where I come from, you don't give people of authority or people you respect a firm handshake. You give them a weak handshake to show deference. When you do this, you are demonstrating they're superior.

Twenty years later, I went to visit Father Bollman, and I explained this to him. "Remember when I gave you a weak handshake? It was a sign of respect." It was an aha moment for him, just like it had been for me.

TO SPEAK UP OR NOT TO SPEAK UP

After graduation, from 2003 to 2004 I worked at a local bank in Cincinnati. I worked as a consumer banking consultant, preparing financial needs analyses for consumer and commercial clients. I provided and serviced credit and debit cards for business and individual accounts, handled customer complaints, and recommended solutions that might better serve clients' personal and business needs.

At one point, the branch manager left. He was replaced with someone new instead of promoting the current assistant manager. I sat between the new manager and the assistant manager. The new branch manager was just out of school; he was young, ambitious, and hardworking but transactional. The assistant manager was equally hardworking and ambitious but a little older and more of a relationship builder. Their different styles sometimes created conflict.

I was close to the assistant manager, because he had been at the branch longer. The new manager's style often didn't sit very well with him, and he would complain and tell me he was getting ready to confront him. I would hear him out, allow him to vent, and then convince him to avoid a confrontation.

People are a bit more direct in their communication here than they are in Ghana. In the United States, it's acceptable to tell your boss that the work he is giving you is too much and you don't have the time or the skills to do it. This is not a very common practice in Africa. In Africa, poverty is widespread, and there are very few jobs. We also embrace an external family structure, where your family extends beyond your wife and kids. If you can afford it, you are responsible for your siblings, your nephews and nieces, and other family members. With the lack of opportunity and the additional responsibility to take care of our extended family, the stakes become so high that you probably don't want to chance losing your job.

There is a joke that Africans answer questions with questions. One day, an American White man set out for Africa to test this theory. When he arrived at the airport, he asked the first African he saw, "I hear Africans answer questions with questions. Is this true?"

The African man said, "Who told you that?"

Africans answer with a question because they want to know where the question is leading. They want to make sure they understand the purpose of the question so they can answer in a way that avoids misinterpretation. They also don't want to miss an economic opportunity if there is one. All this means that we are less likely to speak up to authority, complain, or risk our position.

I eventually moved on to another job, leaving the two of them to deck it out. A few months later, I learned the assistant manager at the bank was fired. I thought to myself, *Maybe he might still have his job if I were there.*

The assistant manager had misunderstood the new culture of the office brought by his nemesis, the new branch manager. It cost him his job.

PERFORMANCE EVALUATION

One time, when I was working at a local bank, it was time for my performance evaluation, and I gave myself lower marks. My boss asked me why I did this, and I told him in Africa, we let our work speak for itself, whereas here we speak for our work. He understood and then raised my marks, because he said I earned them. I found out that in the U.S. we need to speak up for our work.

I wish I'd known that earlier. Unfortunately, one time a friend of mine didn't get a job because I didn't understand the grading system and in my evaluation of her gave her low marks. I felt bad about this, but now that I understand the process, I can navigate it better.

RACE IN AMERICA

A colleague at a bank pointed out a very interesting pattern. There were three of us on the platform side of the bank: the branch manager (a White man), the assistant manager (an African American), and a personal banker (me, an African). The branch was in a low- to medium-income area of town, and our clients would often overdraw their accounts. This would result in overdraft fees, which we could waive. When the customers needed their overdraft fees reversed, they came to me or the other Black banker, and we usually did it. But when these same customers wanted their tax returns prepared or wanted to invest their money, they would go right to the White banker.

Another time when I worked at a bank, the managers thought an immigrant applying for a small business loan was acting suspiciously because he did not make eye contact. I overheard them and explained that in some cultures it is considered rude to look someone in the eye, so maybe the person is showing respect to not make eye contact. I'm not saying my colleagues shouldn't have been suspicious; what I'm saying is give people a chance before you jump to the wrong conclusion.

My bigger take here is we might have lost a business opportunity due to a cultural misunderstanding. If an immigrant is asking for a business loan to grow his business, but not making the expected eye contact, a bank would be leaving a lot of money on the table by being suspicious and choosing not to do business with him. Immigrants own a lot of small businesses in the United States.

I told an African American friend of mine about what happened, and he said even though he is not an immigrant, he is uncomfortable at banks, even when he is taking out money. So, if you have your frontline workers thinking suspiciously about immigrants or people of color, you could be losing money. Maybe some sensitivity training or orientation training is needed so that these things do not continue to happen.

I know racial bias is still a problem in the United States. It's a problem everywhere. If it's not the color of your skin, it's your family name or the province you come from. Whatever makes you different can make you stand out—good or bad. With all cultural differences, the trick is to understand them and look for the opportunities they bring. That might mean an opportunity to bridge cultures or find a niche market.

For the first nine months I was in Cincinnati, I went without a haircut. I just didn't have the money. A haircut cost twelve dollars there compared to only one dollar in Ghana. My afro had been growing for nearly a year. I walked past a barbershop every day on my way to the Chinese restaurant, but I avoided a haircut because it was too expensive. One day, I had a little bit of money in my pocket, so I ventured into the barbershop.

I walked in and saw a White barber, wearing a white jacket and holding a pair of scissors. He asked, "How can I help you?" Sometimes that question means *What do you need?* but sometimes it means *Are you sure you belong here?* I told him I needed a haircut, and he said he didn't know how to cut Black hair.

I stood still for a minute, trying to process what he was saying. This was the first time in my life I ever heard the expression *Black hair*. I didn't understand how the color affected the cut. Hair was hair, wasn't it? Didn't this barber know how to cut hair that is the color black—or didn't he know how to cut Black people's hair? The two of us had a moment of truth during that interaction; we both stared at each other in confusion. I finally turned around and left the shop.

I learned that day that Black people go one place for haircuts, and White people go somewhere else. I'm sure I was the first Black person to walk in this man's barbershop. He was shocked. I was shocked too. It was a good aha moment. He wasn't racist or angry or confrontational; it's just how the system works in this culture. I didn't know any of those dynamics, so I had to learn. One side effect of learning this tidbit, though, was that I now knew that Black people had their own barbershops. I'd learn later that they had their own lines of hair products too. And their own skin products. They were a niche market, ready to embrace the right products for their needs.

LAW ENFORCEMENT

Immigrants face many cultural challenges, and some of them can actually be dangerous. One context where an immigrant can easily be misunderstood in the United States is law enforcement.

For instance, one day a client was having an argument with the bank manager. We were all sitting around and talking, and we turned our attention to the argument. The customer was African American, and the bank manager was White.

For some reason, in the process of arguing, the client attempted to put his hand in his pocket. The bank manager lunged at him, grabbing his arm. The client was surprised and asked why he was being attacked. The manager said, "Never put your hand in your pocket; it can be interpreted as a threat."

I didn't know that. So I asked one of my colleagues, "Why can't he put his hand in his pocket?"

He said, "Because they think you're reaching for a gun, especially if you're Black."

A gun? I wondered why anyone would be carrying a gun around. It wasn't something I'd even think of. I didn't know about this cultural expectation.

And then I read about Amadou Diallo, a twenty-three-year-old Guinean student who was shot nineteen times in New York. He didn't know either. Plainclothes police officers began to question him and asked to see his hands. In his confusion by the situation, Diallo ran back toward his home and also reached in his pocket for his wallet, probably trying to produce an ID. Even at a routine traffic stop, police will ask for an ID. However, if you can't reach in your pocket, how can you show it to them? Immigrants, by and large, don't know they shouldn't reach into their pockets and wouldn't realize it suggests they have a weapon. Most people in Africa and developing countries don't carry guns and are therefore not sensitized to this behavior. But that doesn't safeguard them from the very real dangers of misunderstanding.

The best way to spread this type of cultural interpretation message is through community outreach to immigrant populations. America graciously receives immigrants to the United States in large numbers. This good act should be coupled with training and sensitizing our law enforcement to the broad cultures and the behavior of immigrants. They come with different ways and different expectations.

A government organization ideally could teach immigrants about potential cultural misunderstandings—especially the dangerous ones. Law enforcement could also do their part by reaching out to the immigrant community. The police need to understand that there are things that an immigrant might do that might not necessarily mean what the police expect.

But until such government programs exist, it is up to us as immigrants to learn as much as we can, not only to find a community and build our businesses, but to remain safe. Immigrants need to learn from friends and neighbors what is expected and accepted.

IMMIGRANTS OR AMERICANS?

Some first-generation immigrants want their children to speak their mother language. They make sure their children understand their culture. This is a good thing. Others belong to a different school. In my case, I'm not too worried about teaching my daughter Ghanaian language and customs. I'm more interested in teaching her math and science and the things she needs to live in the country where she is today, because the possibility of going back to Africa and staying there is low.

I ran into a friend and her husband at the Harpers Point Kroger one day. Her husband was complaining that our children—theirs and mine—weren't embracing the Ghanaian culture enough. They were hanging out with Joe and David and Joseph (referring to White people), and he was concerned that he was losing his children. But his wife knows me better. She knows that I am married to a White woman. So she laughed and said, "This is not the right man to talk to about this!"

The question of dual citizenship is an important one. I'm a Ghanaian who became an American citizen. I have a friend who is African

American, and she is thinking of getting a dual citizenship in Ghana. She asked me why I wasn't a dual citizen. I told her my big concern was that if I'm flying and my plane goes down somewhere, which country is going to come for me?

If I'm talking to an African man who was born in the United States—his heritage is African, but he was born in the United States—I speak to him differently than how I'd speak to an African-born person, because I know that his values are a little different from my values. Like my daughter, he was born here; he looks African, but he is American. But if I'm talking to somebody who came to the United States at twenty-five or thirty years old, they'll have different experiences, and we'll communicate differently. I have a friend who's a little bit of both; she came to the United States when she was five years old. Some of the things I expect her to understand, she doesn't, and some of the things I don't expect her to understand, she gets. She's somewhere in between.

From a business perspective, when I'm selling to somebody like my daughter Chelsea who was born here and somebody else who arrived in the United States as an adult, the marketing dynamics are different. Because we are looking at demographics, and we're looking at cultural background, and these two segments are distinct. There are tested ways to communicate with each of them. But there's a new group of people (between five and fifteen years old) who don't necessarily respond to the stimuli and marketing segments of these two segments. And when I'm selling to millennials as opposed to Gen Z, my marketing strategy is different. What might appeal to someone who was born here and is a United States citizen and what might appeal to the second-generation immigrant or someone who arrived later on might not necessarily be the same. From a marketing or recruitment standpoint, this is something you have to be aware of and address in your strategy.

If somebody comes from Ghana to the United States when they are thirty years old, I'm probably not even going to worry about selling them shea butter, because they have ties in Ghana. They almost surely are already familiar with shea butter, and they will either have their family send them some, or when they visit Ghana, they'll come back with a packet of shea butter for themselves.

When I started selling shea butter, I went to the African stores, and they turned me away. They said, "Look, Africans aren't going to buy shea butter." So they're not my demographic. Somebody who was born here, though, will pay a premium price for shea butter because it is foreign to them. This person is very clearly my demographic.

But what about the in-between person, someone who came to the United States at a young age? Some of them might have a relationship to their motherland, though some of them may not. First-generation immigrants weren't born here, but they've been here long enough that they are more or less assimilated Americans. Nobody talks about this hybrid group.

When you're dealing with this group, it can be a little confusing because they have enough experience to have incorporated into American culture, but they still have their roots in another country. They don't act typically or speak like the kids who were born here. But they also don't act like the adults who immigrated at age twenty-five. This is not a group that is often talked about, which makes them a tricky group to market to. But it also means they are a market segment many companies aren't targeting. If you can target them, you may have little competition. And if you belong to this hybrid generation, you have an advantage. You're almost in two worlds. You understand the first-generation immigrants and the local-born Americans, but you also understand your own in-between group. These people are part of my demographic as well.

ACCENT

Clear communication requires that you understand the local culture. But it goes beyond the abstract obstacles of idiom or situational expectations. As an immigrant, sometimes your words simply aren't clear to the local people. Your accent can be a barrier between you and the culture you're living in.

When I first met my former wife, she asked what I studied. I said *finance*, and she thought I said *fine arts*. She wondered why I worked for a Big Four accounting firm with a fine arts degree. Another time, I was getting ready to go out in the morning, and I was looking for my pants. I said, "Where are my khakis?" My wife left the room and came back with my car keys.

Now the lesson is that if I'm trying to build a network or sell a product, people need to understand me. If people are misinterpreting what I'm saying, they may miss out on an opportunity that would benefit us both—or even a friendship. It's not your fault that you have an accent, but it makes it more challenging to get things across. You have to learn how to deal with that and be able to succeed in the society you want to be a part of. How do you communicate clearly if your communication is literally unclear? This is a problem many immigrants face in everyday life, but it is especially important when you are trying to start or run a business.

A while back, I was on a podcast, and one of the questions was "How are you able to survive in corporate America, not only as a Black man but as an immigrant?" I thought about my answer, and my big secret power was simple and obvious: One of the ways I've learned to survive is to slow down. I'm a very fast talker when I'm in my element, but I had to train myself to slow down when I talk. I also had to develop writing skills, where the advantage is there's no accent.

There are other things you can do, of course, like taking speech classes or working with a dialect coach. But simply being mindful of how I'm speaking, slowing down when I talk, and paying attention to whether the other person understands me has helped me get this far. People want to understand you, and if you are able to work together to communicate clearly, you can work together in other ways too.

SETTING UP FOR BUSINESS

While I was working at the bank, I decided to go back to school to get a degree in finance. I figured that going into a more technical area might eliminate some of the cultural challenges I faced in sales and marketing. I went back to Xavier and got an MBA in finance. I figured that two plus two equals four wherever you are, regardless of your cultural differences.

Around this time, I began paying back the loan Father Bollman had given me. Every month, I would mail a check to the church, somewhere around three hundred dollars a month. One day, I stopped by the church to say hello to Father Bollman and thank him again for the loan. He told me the church had been receiving payments from someone and wanted to know if they were from me. I said yes. He told me to immediately stop making payments on the loan. He forgave it right then in another generous gesture.

When I graduated with my finance degree, I found a job with PricewaterhouseCoopers (PwC). I worked at their Cincinnati office as a financial analyst from 2004 to 2006. At the time, Procter & Gamble had just purchased Gillette, and PwC was helping P&G with the merger. I was hired as an analyst to work on the integration process.

With every step of my American dream in motion, it was time to build something for myself, to create my own path. I had made it to the United States, earned two MBAs, and gained experience with some very successful companies. I'd even begun building business bridges between the United States and Africa, even if it was for someone else's company. Now it was time to step out on my own. PwC gave me my first financial analysis skills, which gave me the training I needed to begin building my own business. I began preparing financial projections for my business plan. The ability to provide strong financial projections would enable me to get investors. Even friends want to see reports and projections to make sure their investment is good. I learned how to do all this at PwC. Now, I had to figure out what business to build.

4

STARTING A BUSINESS

In 2016, I was working at JPMorgan Chase as a consultant, and my friend Chris invited me to his friend Greg's house just to hang out. When we got to the house, Chris introduced me. Greg asked me the million-dollar question most immigrants get asked: "Where are you from?"

I said, "I'm from Ghana."

Greg's eyes got big, and he said, "Hold on," and ran off while I wondered what I did wrong. A minute later, he re-emerged with a huge bowl of shea butter in his hands.

I was confused. What was an African American doing with a bowl of shea butter at 10:00 p.m. in Columbus, Ohio?

I asked him, "What are you doing with this?"

"I sell it," he said. "This is my business."

I looked at him in surprise. Back home in Ghana, we have so much shea butter; it's everywhere. I never thought anybody would buy it in the United States. When you have so much of something, you just take it for granted. I had to come all this way to the United States—to Columbus, Ohio—to hear about shea butter from an African American who was selling the product.

The next morning, I thought, *Hmm, you know what? Let me put my MBA to the test.* So I got up, turned my laptop on, and googled the market size of shea butter in the United States. *Wow!* A light bulb went off, and I thought, *Oh, that's why he had such a big bowl of shea butter.* Sometimes you have to go backward to go forward; it looked like my home might be the key to my future.

SELLING SHEA BUTTER

After my position ended with JPMorgan Chase, I returned to Cincinnati and found another job, this time with Duke Energy as a financial analyst. By now, I also was buying shea butter from Greg in Columbus and selling it in Cincinnati. I started selling shea butter at churches, flea markets, and festivals on nights and weekends. I began selling to my colleagues in the office, and I picked up a few customers along the way. I would sometimes travel in the evening to Columbus to sell shea butter and might sell only fifty dollars' worth of products. Columbus is about ninety minutes away from Cincinnati, and I needed more than fifty dollars just in gas money to make the trip. I was losing money at some of these events, but I said to myself, *You're just learning the business and building awareness.*

I decided to start building connections in the Black churches in Cincinnati, since most of my customers were African American. Because I was not originally from Cincinnati, I asked some of my friends to provide me with the names of the top ten African American churches in the city. Armed with this list, I started attending these churches and began selling products at some of them after the service; when they had events, they started inviting me to sell. I was also selling shea butter to my neighbors in the Harpers Point Kroger store parking lot with the dream of seeing my products make it onto the store's shelves one day. I sold shea butter to anybody who would buy it.

My sales began to pick up, so I was buying more and more products from Greg. The sales grew so rapidly that they exceeded Greg's capacity to produce. One day, he told me the production process was too tedious, and he stopped producing for me and asked me to produce my own products. I still work with Greg—he is my biggest advocate and one of my distributors in Columbus.

At this time I was also selling African black soap, a mixture made from plantain skin and shea butter. At a festival in Columbus, a White kid walked up to our table and started checking out the products. He picked up the black soap and asked me if White people could use it as well. I said, "Yes, it's good for everybody!"

Later I asked myself why it is called *black soap*. Is it because it's black? Not all black soap is even black. This was a small lesson in marketing.

BASEMENT OPERATIONS

With my Columbus supply chain lost, I decided to buy imported shea butter from Ghana, and I started my own shea butter factory in my basement. Many years earlier, our basement had flooded and we had done some restoration work. After fixing the flood damage, we couldn't afford carpeting, so we left the floor bare. This unfinished basement made for a good shea butter production center.

Before the second time I received a shipment of raw shea butter from Ghana, I looked into getting a broker, but this service cost more than I could afford. In fact, the broker fees were more than the cost of the shea butter. I decided to go out on my own again and try my luck. When I arrived at the airport to clear my products, I met the same White customs agent who had recommended I get a broker

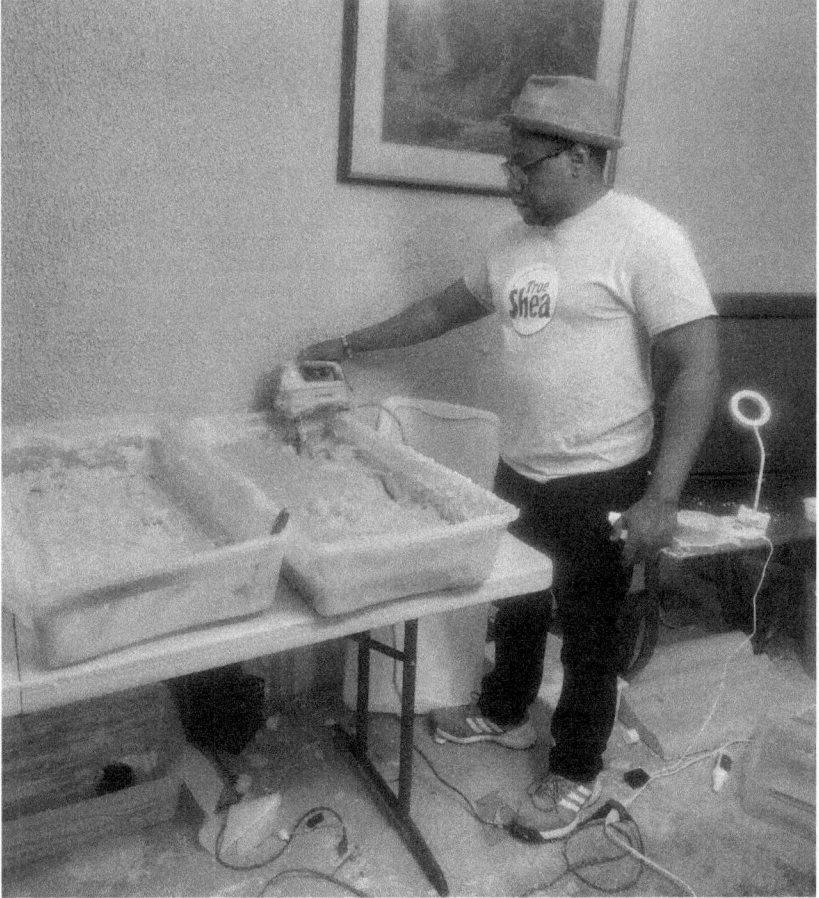

While True Shea is now a professionally processed product and sold across the U.S., Manny's early years in business involved a hand mixer, materials from home, and a lot of hard work to create the product.

when I picked up my first shipment, and he scolded me again for not getting one. The third time, I again went to the airport without a broker, but this time, the gentleman was there with an African female officer, so I joined the line for her inspection. A significant portion of our customers are African American women, so I gambled that she might know what shea butter is and would be more lenient with me. Lo and behold, she cleared the products for me with no problem at all. We eventually became friends, and I made sure she was working before I went to clear my products, even if it meant waiting for days.

At this point, my sales had picked up, and so the basement operation also had to pick up speed. When I received a shipment, I had to rent a U-Haul truck at 8:00 a.m. to go to the airport to clear my products. I was now receiving one ton of shea butter at a time. This consisted of fifty large boxes, which I had to load into the U-Haul before going to work at Duke Energy. At the end of my workday, I'd go home, unload the boxes into my basement, and then return the truck before 4:00 p.m. so I wouldn't be charged for going beyond my eight-hour rental.

Fortunately, today we transport our shea butter in a full container through a seaport in New Jersey, and I am no longer responsible for this process. That first customs agent would be proud!

TESTING AND SAMPLING

My family was very helpful in testing my products in the very early stages. I would get my daughter, Chelsea, who was then about eight years old, to help me with the texture and fragrances. She and her mother, Molly, were my first testers. I started by selling unscented shea butter. After a while, my customers started asking for scented products, so I went online and found a company that sells fragrances for skincare. I bought samples of the twenty bestselling fragrances and started sharing them with my family and friends—at work, over Thanksgiving dinner, at coffee shops—to determine which they liked best. This focus group study chose kiwi, vanilla, and lavender, which we still sell to this day.

As Chelsea got older, she started helping me during her free time. She would assist with testing the shea butter and labeling the jars, two tasks she and her mom still take on; those two ladies have perfected this skill. They gave me initial feedback on both the texture of the shea butter and the scents I used for each of my products. Their advice was priceless, but I also looked for feedback from others. I began carrying shea butter everywhere I went, sharing samples at my doctor's office, barbershops, and churches.

LET THE SHELF DECIDE

When you're just starting out, don't get lost in the details. Sometimes the more you know—about your product, its market share, the customer, and so on—the more time you spend learning more. Don't try to get the product perfect before testing the market. That's how you miss out on an opportunity. Instead, get it into the customer's hands. Once it has arms and legs, let it move. Let the shelf decide.

Free samples are a staple part of that decision. You know you have a good product when someone tries it out and then comes back and pays for the product. However you think a product is going to perform on the shelf, the reality may be completely different. But once you receive payment for the product, then you have product validation. The shelf has decided. If it sells, then you know.

Product knowledge, industry knowledge, research, and market knowledge are all important. But entrepreneurship is about doing. The only way to grow is by doing. Don't sit and wait and do research. You have to act.

As my business continued to pick up, I decided to approach a store named Jungle Jim's. This is a local but well-respected international market that draws customers from around the region. There are two of these stores in Cincinnati. They sell lots of products from all around the world, so it's more like a sightseeing adventure for some customers. One day, I approached the manager in the health and beauty section and said, "Hey, I have some shea butter. Would you like some to try?"

After two or three tries, she referred me to the international section, because she figured my products best belonged there. I called the international department a few times, wanting to speak to the manager, without any luck. One day, I called and someone finally answered. He asked how he could help me.

I told him I was looking for the manager, and he said he was not the manager but again asked whether he could help me himself. I told him I produced shea butter and wanted to know if he was interested. He invited me to meet with him, and he asked me what differentiated my product from the other shea butter products out there.

I told him, "Our product is whipped, making it very easy to use." I had just spent eighteen hours whipping shea butter over the weekend, making it ultrasoft.

He asked me to bring twelve jars for him to try. Because of my day job, I delivered them over the weekend. At the time, I thought, *I have to drive fifty miles to supply only twelve jars!* But a month later, he asked me to bring twenty-four jars. And two months after that, he asked for forty-eight jars.

Three months later, Jungle Jim's asked for one hundred jars, and not long after that, they asked for five hundred jars. The numbers just kept increasing. Pretty soon, I was selling in both Jungle Jim's locations. At that point, I thought, *Okay, I think I must be on to something now. This product has legs.*

I approached their Herb 'N Jungle department to sell them my fragrance products. They loved those too. This department was extremely helpful to me. They put my products on display and even featured them on a screen during Black History Month.

As the business continued to grow and to reach out further from my home base in Cincinnati, we ventured into the Dayton market. I walked into a store called Health Foods Unlimited and shared some samples with the manager, a woman named Rhonda Miller. She asked me to bring her twelve jars. I told her that Dayton was quite a distance from Cincinnati, and I would appreciate a bigger order to make it worth the trip. She was initially reluctant but went ahead anyway. Health Foods Unlimited is an all-natural store, and since our products are all natural, our business picked up really quickly there. We still do a lot of business with them today.

I went from twelve jars to five hundred jars at Jungle Jim's and was selling similar numbers at Health Foods Unlimited. I am grateful to these two stores for trusting me and my product. Jungle Jim's was the first retail store that put me on the shelf. Although they are a relatively small company in Cincinnati, they're big enough to be respected. Everybody in Cincinnati knows Jungle Jim's; it's an iconic store. The success at both Jungle Jim's and Health Foods Unlimited gave me the experience and confidence to approach Kroger, which is where True Shea really took off.

PART 2

SCALING INTO KROGER

In my experience, there are three factors that determine your ability to scale: your connections with people, manufacturing, and funding. These pieces go hand in hand; you can't do any of them without the others.

Without people, you have no one to buy your product, no one to put it on shelves, and no one to talk to about how to grow your business. Your connections include networking, of course, but they also include knowing who can help you through each stage of your business growth. They include mentors who add to your expertise with their own, and they even include the way you share information with others.

Once you have your product in a few local stores, it's time to jump into a bigger market. You'll need connections within that market to help you grow. For them to invest in your product, they must love it. And if they love it, they're going to want a *lot* of it. That means you can't continue manufacturing on your own, in your basement. You're going to need partners with the manufacturing skills and equipment to produce your product at scale.

Finally, you'll need money to do any of this. You'll need investors who believe in what you are doing and who are willing to provide capital to help you do it. But you'll also need customers to buy your product, which means effective marketing.

5

CONNECTIONS

I n 2018, I was selling products in the two Jungle Jim's locations, Health Foods Unlimited, and a few other stores. With that momentum, I approached Kroger to see if they were interested in buying my products. Now, you have to understand, Kroger is a major grocery retailer, with more than twenty-seven hundred stores in the United States. So, I had to jump through more hoops than I did for Jungle Jim's if True Shea was going to land on their shelves. But the payoff would be putting my product within the reach of thousands of new customers.

Kroger makes a conscious effort to connect with diversity businesses through their Supplier Diversity and Inclusion program. I approached their supplier diversity director at the time to show off the product and to learn how to do business with this retail giant. My goal for this meeting was to gather information about the process, the departments, and the products Kroger sold within the program, as well as the application process. I learned all of that and so much more. It was the first time I heard terms such as *broker, category manager,* and *P10,* which means some kind of calendar month. All of this was really confusing.

WHAT IS A BROKER?

In my earlier experience, I had come across the term *broker.* In Ghana, we also called this a clearing agent—someone who clears your goods from the harbor. But what Kroger meant by the term was something completely different. The broker is the person who helps a vendor (like me or you) prepare for a meeting with a large retailer. They help you determine with whom you should meet at the retailer, and they help you to do business with them afterward. They act as a kind of middleman between you and the retailer.

You cannot successfully do business with any major retailer without a broker. The best way to find one is to ask your retailer. If you have a company that you want to work with, whether that's Kroger or Target, contact the supply manager at that company. They can give you the names of recommended brokers for their particular retail area. This will give you the advantage of working with a broker who already has a relationship with the retailer; *their* foot in the door gets *your* foot in the door.

But it's not always that easy. It takes time and perseverance to find a broker to help scale your business. Not every broker will take you on. Some will even want to interview you, because they want to ensure that you are a valuable partner. They work on commission. They make money when you make money, so if you are not positioned to make money, taking you on as a client is a waste of their time. You have to be prepared, know your stuff, and be ready to show how your product and business plan are poised for success. Once you have a broker on board, they'll help connect you with the retailer, even delivering product to them. And then you won't be like me, renting a giant U-Haul and picking up tons of product every few weeks!

Kroger's supplier diversity manager made it clear that I needed to get a broker and gave me a list of brokers to call. I called almost all of the brokers on the list, but none of them would answer my calls. One day, I was meeting with one of my mentors, Brad Trucksis, in search of a contract manufacturer to help produce our products. He introduced me to one of his acquaintances who owned a manufacturing company. The manufacturer could not help me, but he introduced us to somebody he knew. So Brad and I met with Dave Slusher, only to find out he was a vice president at one of the largest brokers for Kroger. Dave introduced me to broker Bryan Whitaker, who worked with us until we got into Kroger and, later on, worked for me as our operations manager. It's all about connections!

BE THE *WHATEVER YOUR PRODUCT IS* GUY

While working with the broker, I was still independently working my supplier diversity channel. One day, during the gala for the Ohio Minority Supply Development Council (OMSDC), I saw the Kroger supplier diversity director and introduced myself to her. She smiled and shook my hand, then kept on shaking it with a blank look in her eyes as I tried to tell her who I was. Despite having had several conversations with her by that point, she did not recognize me. It was a bit embarrassing to have this happen in front of everybody—for both of us.

As our extended handshake was becoming unbearable, the director's assistant walked in and gave me a big hug. With some relief, I told her that her boss didn't remember me, and she looked surprised. I could see her thinking to herself, *You don't remember him? We've been talking to Manny for months!*

At that point, the crowd was moving into the gala, and my director and her assistant drifted off to the bathroom. I wandered into the main event hall feeling embarrassed. A few minutes later, they came back from the bathroom, and the director walked straight toward me.

I thought to myself, *What do I do now?*

She said, "Why didn't you say you were the shea butter guy?"

We both laughed and talked some more, and the tension eased. I didn't know they had a name for me in the office! The director asked me to follow up with her on Monday, which led to my first meeting with a category manager. Even an awkward, embarrassing connection can lead to something good.

PERSEVERING CONNECTIONS

Unfortunately, Kroger's annual product review—when they decide which products will be purchased for the next year—had just ended, so I had to wait for another year. At the same time, Kroger went through a major restructuring, which affected all my contacts, and I had to start all over again making connections.

Not too long later, a new supplier diversity director was appointed. I needed to build a relationship with this person from scratch, so I reached out to another mentor, Carl Satterwhite, who introduced me to Angel Colon, a man who would later become my greatest cheerleader, coach, and advocate. At my first meeting with him, we were actually joined by the board chairman of the Ghana Export Promotion Authority, who was in town visiting me.

Angel also brought his assistant to the meeting. She and I had worked together at the same bank ten years earlier. This accidental connection—my previous relationship with her—really helped my business. She took the time to engage with me and learn about my business. When the next annual product review came around, she was instrumental in getting me a meeting. And she did something that has stuck with me to this day: The review was on her day off, but she came to the office anyway to make sure it went well for me.

At the meeting, I met the category manager and her team. The review went well. She really liked the texture of our shea butter. At the time, I was still making the shea in my basement, and because I knew I was going in for a big presentation, I whipped that shea butter with extra love. It was extra soft and easy to apply. We also shared our small but fast-growing sales volumes with her.

After the review, she said, "I like the texture of your product." She then added jokingly, "But your packaging is not coming into my store." Bear in mind that we were still selling the products in deli containers. So our next problem was to find a different packaging solution. Unfortunately, the product review happens only once a year, so we had to wait for another twelve months to get our product on the shelves.

WHAT IS A CATEGORY MANAGER?

Category managers work in the retail world, where they find, market, and evaluate products and merchandise for companies. They review products, evaluate suppliers, and develop merchandising initiatives with vendors and suppliers. They work in various retail categories, including clothing, food, beauty supply, and so on, and they examine the aspects of merchandising. This could include the evaluation of supplies or maintenance of levels of inventory or determining whether a product might be a good fit for their store.

A category manager is like a buyer, except that some category managers take more responsibility for their category. Rather than a simple transactional relationship, they take ownership of their category. They might even develop vendors, helping them become more professional and grow, like Kroger did with me.

MENTORSHIP

I mentioned a couple of my mentors earlier, and I cannot express how important these relationships can be. Mentorship is key because you will learn from your mentors much more than you could on your own, and your network often immediately expands to include theirs. They can answer questions—even questions you don't know you should ask. They share their own mistakes, so you don't have to make them yourself. Most of all, they can advocate for you. For me, getting into major retailers, especially into Kroger, required people who already had connections there and could call these organizations on my behalf. They introduced me to people or helped me set up meetings. It can take an act of God to get a meeting, but my mentors helped me connect with the right people.

I have already mentioned Carl Satterwhite; another crucial supporter was Steve Hightower. They both are very successful and influential Black businessmen in Cincinnati, but they have been generous with their time and advice. When I was producing shea butter in my basement, I asked them, "Should I get a loan and build a small factory on my own, or should I outsource it?"

Both options have advantages: When you own the factory, you might have a loan, but the cost of production is lower. If you choose to outsource, you don't have loan payments, but the cost of production is a little higher. How to handle manufacturing is a difficult decision that warrants a whole chapter later in this book, but these two mentors each told me without hesitation, "Don't touch manufacturing. Go to a contract manufacturer. Do not manufacture your own." And I think that is the best advice I ever got.

Although my mentors have been extremely generous, their advice did not come from a chance meeting; I have built strong relationships with each of them. Relationship building, which is a key part of mentorship, is like going on a date. You don't just go up to a person and say, "I want you to date me." If you do that, you probably won't see them again. I have between thirty and forty people I consider mentors; I've never asked anybody to mentor me, but I do ask for their advice. It happens organically, through the relationships you build.

First of all, it's important that you demonstrate to the people with whom you want to work that you know what you are talking about, that you're a serious businessperson.

I first ran into Carl Satterwhite at the Harpers Point Kroger grocery store, a store I frequent about ten times a week. I knew him from afar because he's a public figure, but he didn't know me. One day, I went to Kroger and saw him in an aisle. I thought to myself, *This guy looks like Carl Satterwhite.* So I went up to him.

I said, "Carl?"

He looked up and said, "Yeah?"

"Hey, my name is Manny. I heard you speak at 'Unpolished' at Crossroads Church. I own a skincare line, and I'm trying to get into Kroger."

Now, this is a very, very busy man, but anybody who hears *Kroger* is probably going to pay attention to what you're saying: "I'm trying to get into stores" is vague and implies that you're just getting started. "Getting into Kroger" is a concrete and ambitious plan.

And then I dropped another name. "I've been working with people like Steve Hightower. He is my mentor." This is crucial—I wasn't lying or simply name-dropping. This was the truth. Steve Hightower is one of the most successful diversity business owners in the Cincinnati area, and I know him very well.

Carl stopped shopping. He focused on me as though he might be thinking, *Okay, this is something I probably want to hear about.* We talked for a little bit. Eventually, he told me he was at the store to get chicken for dinner and needed to get home. I thanked him for his time and asked for his business card.

It was only a five-minute conversation, but it got the ball rolling. I sent him a follow-up email about what I was doing and how I was doing it. And I said I'd like to have a meeting with him.

So Carl invited me to Queen City Club, a prestigious private club in Cincinnati, for lunch. I'd never been there; I didn't even know that type of place existed. But it was the kind of place where you might see CEOs and professional football players laughing over drinks.

After some small talk, Carl asked, "Have you spoken to OMSDC?" (That's the Ohio Minority Supply Development Council, if you remember.)

I said, "Yes, I have."

Then he asked, "Do you have a certification?"

I said, "I'm certified with them."

"Have you spoken with Kroger about this?"

I had. Everything he asked me, I had already done or was working on—check, check, check, check, check.

Before he offered a specific way to help me, he wanted to make sure I was serious, organized, and proactive. He wanted to make sure I was working toward my goal. Once he knew I was on the ball, he said, "Okay, you've done all the things I was going to ask you. What can I do?"

"I want you to introduce me to the main supply director at Kroger."

That was a big ask, and we both knew it. He said, "Okay, I got you. I'm going to do the introduction."

And he made the introduction, as simple as that. It was an easy thing for him to do, but it wouldn't have happened without us first beginning to build a relationship. Part of that was me building trust by showing him I knew what I was talking about first and foremost.

So, do your homework! And don't waste their time—or your own. Don't set up a meeting only to ask the obvious. If the information is on the internet, you should already have it. Go to the meeting well prepared.

Mentorship offers crucial benefits you could never access on your own, but it's a two-way street. To repay the kindness and support your mentors show you, once you have established yourself, give that same support to newer business owners. I have learned from my mentees just as I have from my mentors. Sharing your knowledge with the next generation can be extremely rewarding. That's part of the reason I'm writing this book: to help more immigrant business owners than I could ever meet with in person.

AFRICAN EXPORT-IMPORT BANK (AFREXIMBANK)

The African Export-Import Bank (AFREXIMBANK) finances and promotes trade with and within Africa. I was fortunate to attend the AFREXIMBANK annual meetings and their thirtieth anniversary celebration in Ghana in June of 2023. This event brought together key African and Caribbean leaders and senior executives across multiple spheres.

The event was very well organized and attended by some of the most influential people on the continent of Africa, including Professor Benedict Oramah, president and chairman of AFREXIMBANK, who delivered a compelling speech urging intra-African trade between member nations. Other attendees and speakers included the president of Ghana, Nana Addo Dankwa Akufo-Addo, and Aliko Dangote, the world's richest Black person and the richest person in Africa.

At this event, I met my high school friend Mr. Sebastian Ashong-Katai, who is the group head for Financial Institutions and International Organizations at Ecobank Transnational Incorporated. I shared with him my aspirations to collaborate with AFREXIMBANK to promote business between Africa and the U.S. He gladly introduced me to Ms. Oluranti Doherty, the director of Export Development and acting director of Advisory and Capital Markets. At this meeting, I shared with Ms. Oluranti Doherty that I had successfully exported shea butter products from Ghana and had placed them in 1,500 Kroger stores and was looking to help other African companies export their products to the U.S. She admired the accomplishment and subsequently introduced me to various key associates at AFREXIMBANK to help me in this effort. Both Mr. Sebastian Ashong-Katai and Ms. Oluranti Doherty continue to be a great resource for me by continuously introducing me to key players and resources.

COMMUNICATION

During the second year of waiting for the next annual review at Kroger, I finally found a good-looking jar. Next I had to get new labels printed. I had been printing the labels at home, and that wouldn't work anymore. I found a professional labeling company and told them I needed labels for a potential order at Kroger. They knew how big a deal it was to get into Kroger, and they were extremely excited for me.

I took this year to prepare my business. I began talking to potential investors. I visited a few contract manufacturers just in case the order came through. I continued growing my sales and added smaller stores and hair salons to my customer base. But I kept in touch with my connections at Kroger: I would send emails to the category manager and the supplier diversity team, telling them about the growth of my company and any changes or updates in the industry. I am very much known for sending emails and copying everybody.

Communication—and even overcommunication—is crucial to building a business. First, you want to overcommunicate to all your mentors, investors, prospective investors, category managers, and all your other partners, just to keep them in the loop. I overcommunicate so much that in the last three years, I have barely had any of my investors ever ask me what's going on with the company. Not a month goes by without me firing off emails. It keeps everybody informed so there's nothing they don't already know about me. This creates trust and reassurance and lets them know I'm steering the business in the right direction.

For the category manager, it just makes the conversation a little easier. In one meeting, one of the supplier diversity managers at Kroger made the comment that "Manny has taught me that overcommunication works." It's true—I'm bombarding him. But he never needs to ask me anything because he already knows. Every month, I send something. This keeps me top of mind with all my people. They don't forget me or my product.

Communicating Issues

Communication also helps head off issues before they become problems. When surprises happen, the first thing you want to do is let them know. Get on top of it. Get ahead of it fast. They're going to find out, and it should come from you first. For example, when I had manufacturing issues early on, I sent an email to the Kroger category manager to let them know immediately that we might not be able to meet the demand as quickly as we had hoped. They could then adjust their planning so they weren't left with a half-empty shelf if I came up short.

Finally, we had the second annual review. The category manager was still on board, and the new packaging was right on target. Kroger signed us up; True Shea would be in their stores!

But the sailing is never smooth in business. When I got the contract from Kroger, I had initially said my product was 100 percent shea butter. But when we went into production, we realized that the contract manufacturers did not have the kind of machines to be able to produce 100 percent shea butter, because it's too thick, too high viscosity. So we had to mix it with a little bit of sunflower oil. When you're dealing with a company like Kroger, how do you let them know you're changing the formulation? I had to, of course. I had to go back to the category manager to let her know that I couldn't deliver what I told her I was going to deliver. This was about ten days before my product was due to go on the shelf. Because of the magnitude of the news, I didn't tell her in an email. I asked her out for lunch. In the middle of the meal, I mentioned the problem.

"Manny," she said, "you are lucky you did not tell me this over the phone." If I had done that, she said, they would have pulled my product. That would have been the end of True Shea at Kroger. Instead, I was right there in front of her, being honest and letting her know we had a problem. That honesty won me some leeway, but I also told her we had a solution at the same time.

Part of building relationships is communicating with honesty and vulnerability, and you have to make sure that it's in person. You're building a relationship with the business and with the person helping you work with that business. It's necessary to break bread to have such conversations.

Overpromise, Over-Deliver

Under-promise, over-deliver is a model that works for mainstream America. It means you create goodwill by creating expectations you can easily exceed. But as a diversity businessperson, as an immigrant, even as a woman, *under-promise, over-deliver* doesn't work. When you show up at a meeting or you show up to present, the color of your skin or your accent or whatever makes you not mainstream can immediately make people think that you are not qualified for the job. Anything that makes you stand out can be a strike against you.

If you under-promise, you don't get the shot. You have to prove not only that you can produce the product or do the job, but also that you can overcome whatever perceptions they have about you. Do you think you can under-promise in that situation? No way. You can't even get in the door with that.

For diversity businesses or anybody who's not mainstream, you have to overpromise, then you overwork, and finally you over-deliver. You set their expectations high, promising more than your competition can. Then you exceed those expectations. Yes, it means you must work harder, but there's no room for error. You can't work forty hours of that promise; you must work eighty hours. That's the deal. You overpromise, over-deliver—every time.

Caution: If you can't overwork, please don't overpromise.

When I told Kroger I was ready, I literally was not ready. That was my overpromise. If I had told them I wasn't ready, I wouldn't have had the opportunity to deliver. And frankly, no one is ever ready until they actually take the shot.

True Shea is sold in Kroger stores across the U.S., affording Manny the opportunity to scale up his product through their supplier diversity programs and reach a wider market.

The day I walked out the door with a contract, I started working ninety hours a week, eighteen hours a day. I called all my investors. I said, "We've got a contract from Kroger, but it's a huge problem. I don't know how to deliver." Some of my mentors were surprised that I put so much pressure on myself.

One of my panicky calls was to Steve Hightower. I had asked him to invest in the opportunity, and he helped me, but at the time, he wasn't able to give me all the funding I needed. When he realized that, even without his funding, I was able to put a product on the shelf, he said I lit a fire without matches. This is someone who built his company from scratch as a janitor cleaning bathrooms, and he's at about $500 million in revenue now.

Overpromising is easy. But remember, you also have to over-deliver with this strategy. You light that fire under yourself before getting the matches. I was eventually able to over-deliver on the first Kroger order, but committing to that constant and hard work was crucial to getting it done. The contract isn't the end; it's the beginning.

Build the Connection—and Maintain It

I knew one of my investors, Pierre, for about ten years before he invested in me. I kept him updated both on the business and our friendship for almost a decade. I went to his house and helped him clean the carpet in his basement when it flooded, just as you would with any friend. You're building relationships so that when the opportunity comes, the connection is already there. When some people have a conversation that doesn't pan out, they forget about that person and leave them behind. You don't want to do that. You want to keep that relationship going, even if it's just touching base once a year.

It's important to cultivate those relationships, because you never know what will happen later. I never thought that Pierre, the owner of an engineering company, would come to my rescue. But I knew that he was a businessperson, and he was my mentor and a friend and a spiritual leader—all of which are just as valuable if we never worked together. All these pieces—building relationships, mentoring and being mentored, and overcommunicating while you overpromise and over-deliver—are crucial aspects of creating connections.

6

MANUFACTURING

Now I was at a crossroads. I had this great opportunity from Kroger. They loved my product, and we had new packaging that would work for them. But they wanted LOTS of product. I needed to figure out how to grow my business to manufacture the product in the large quantities that Kroger would put on its shelves. I had to find a new way to manufacture True Shea, or I would spend the whole year in my basement. At this point, I needed to scale my business from five stores to 330 stores in a year. I needed help.

START SCRAPPY

When you start a business, you need to use tactics before you introduce strategy. I'm saying this because, in the beginning, I wasn't using any scientific method. I was just mixing shea butter in my basement and getting the opinions of my daughter and my wife and my friends and family. I'd simply ask, "Hey, what do you think? Give me your opinion real quick." Then I put the product in a deli container and hit the streets to sell it. I was scrappy in the very beginning: no real market research, no pretty jars and labels, just shea butter in a deli container. I used my credit cards and tried to stay afloat. I started small, selling in churches, selling to people on the street. In the beginning, I had a business plan in my head, but I didn't have anything written down.

You have to start by using tactics, but you grow into strategy. At first, it's 100 percent tactics. As your company begins to grow, you begin to trade off some of your tactics for strategy. As your product starts getting attention from bigger stores, you need real data to show to whoever your growth partner is. You need to be packaged a certain way to be able to fit into a large retailer. You need to put together a strategic business plan, because you're going to need money from equity investors or banks. So, midway, you'll be 50 percent tactics, 50 percent strategy. When you get to the Procter & Gamble level, you are full-blown strategy.

Too much education or experience can get in your way in the beginning, and it can be hard to be scrappy. We are taught in business school and corporate America that your venture has to be perfect in order to succeed. But if you wait until your product is perfect, it won't get created. And you can't succeed if you never make or sell anything.

If you work with Fortune 500 companies, you have to have all your data, all your market research ready to go. You need clear backup for your idea and your plan before you even pitch an idea. But that kind of perfectionism in the beginning of a small business doesn't allow you to take off. Your plane—your idea—is on the ground forever. Universities are teaching entrepreneurship, but some are teaching it from a textbook standpoint—without the crucial, real-world hustle.

Because all you need is tactics in the beginning, many successful entrepreneurs don't have any higher education at all. If you can slap together a product and a way to sell it, you don't need a string of letters after your name; all you need is scrappiness. But as you begin to grow, and as you begin to drop some of the tactics and bring in that strategy, it might mean getting an MBA or hiring someone with an MBA to help you fly the plane now that it's on the runway ready for takeoff.

Of course, five- and ten-year strategic plans have their place, but this is farther down the road as you are growing. I am fortunate because I'm good at both strategy and tactics. I'm a hustler, but I still have an MBA and twenty years in corporate America. I've worked with six Fortune 500 companies. Most people don't have the hustle and the corporate experience and education at the same time, but I do. That means I can navigate both the early and late stages of business, but if you have to choose one, choose scrappy.

If I had not been scrappy in the beginning, I would have lost the contract when I ran into my initial problems with the yearly review and then with packaging. A ten-year strategy would not have helped me find a label designer or mix a thousand jars of shea butter. I needed to think fast and find a solution to scale my product. A strategic plan is very important, don't get me wrong. But first, you need to scale fast. Be scrappy first, then build up the polish; the strategy can come later.

However, even as you grow more sophisticated, keep the scrappiness you had early on. Even with a ten-year strategy, there will be crises that will require you to think fast on your feet, and you can't use a strategy in that moment. If your product needs to be on the shelf in two weeks, you have to go back to scrappy and get it done. You can't pause and look at building a five-year strategic plan while the shelves are empty. That's how you lose a contract.

Stay scrappy, even when you have the polish. This applies to every-thing. If you want to make progress, you have to allow yourself the ability to make mistakes, to not be perfect. Staying scrappy builds that improvisational skill, and it keeps you from becoming complacent.

A HEADLESS CHICKEN

After our success with the second yearly product review, Kroger gave us 330 stores to start with. We have an old adage in Ghana: "Cooking for five people is different than cooking for fifty people." I had no idea how I was going to make so much product. I did have a broker at the time: Harlow-HRK. And fortunately, I had some supply chain experience from my work at Cintas Corporation. All that was helpful, but I still needed to raise money and find a manufacturer. I was running around like a chicken without a head. It was a big leap for me, and I knew I had to find a solution—fast!

My options were to set up a factory of my own to produce shea butter or to find a contract manufacturer to produce it for me.

If I stuck to in-house manufacturing, we would have to produce the product ourselves. That meant we could control the manufacturing process to ensure the finished product was great. There would be a low per-unit cost of production, and we could maintain quality control. But it also meant we'd have to take out a loan. We'd owe the bank a significant amount of money. Starting up a good manufacturing facility can run into the $1 million range. I'd need to pledge my personal assets—such as my house—as collateral. I'd also have to manage employees, the manufacturing facility, and the production process.

Contract manufacturing, on the other hand, would require looking for a copacker to manufacture the products for us. This would transfer the manufacturing headache to someone else, and I could focus on my core competency, which is business development and selling products to major retailers. It would mean low debt exposure, and I'd have multiple manufacturers to choose from. But we'd have to rely on this manufacturing partner to produce the right product and deliver on time. It would mean constraints on our potential scaling opportunities, because we'd have to rely on the manufacturer's existing capacity. It would also mean a higher cost of production, because manufacturing adds a markup for the work.

As I mentioned, after consulting with my mentors, I concluded it was best to stay with my core competency of business development to grow the topline and transfer the manufacturing process to the experts. So I started hunting for a contract manufacturer.

Cincinnati is the global headquarters of Procter & Gamble, one of the largest skincare companies in the world. I assumed that finding a contract manufacturer in Cincinnati would be relatively easy. I thought that if I could mix shea butter in my basement, any manufacturer should be able to do that, too. When I started, I was producing about twenty jars a weekend, but I finally got up to speed to produce four hundred jars a weekend. I thought any manufacturer could surely outpace that number in no time.

I didn't know where to start, so I started calling manufacturers in the Yellow Pages. I found one that made shea butter. This company was already producing shea butter lotion for big companies like P&G, so they could surely help me, right? Well, I gave them my formulation and asked them to replicate it and scale it. After several weeks, they were still trying to figure it out in the lab. However, because they were set up for lotion, they couldn't mix my product. Lotion has lower viscosity, and theirs had very little shea butter in it. The unrefined shea butter cream that I make is very thick. It's a completely different ball game. They couldn't scale it.

All this time, I was thinking, *What's wrong with these people? I can make it in my basement without any science background. Why can't they get this with all their chemists?* I didn't have time to waste; Kroger was waiting for the product. Finally, I told them, "You guys have to figure this out. I'm running behind on my deadline for Kroger!"

At this point, I literally had less than four weeks to fix this problem. The president of the manufacturing company and I had become acquaintances by then. I was in his factory every day of the week. He started joking with me, saying, "You sold a product to Kroger that you don't know how to produce?"

And I said, "You're damn right I did." We all joked about it, and it's funny now. But at that point, I was getting worried and needed some humor to cope with the situation. I had a lot of sleepless nights. I'd been waiting for this opportunity for the past three years. I *had* to find a solution.

They finally got the formulation right in their lab. The next step was to move it to the factory floor for production. Then came the next problem. The blades in their big mixing tank were not meant for the viscosity of our shea butter. Remember, if it's not mixed with oil, shea butter can be very thick; I had broken twenty cake mixers in my home factory.

I was getting desperate. I was walking around the streets of Cincinnati asking any pedestrian, cop, and dog whether they knew of a contract manufacturer, and I still could not find one. I went to New York, Chicago, Dallas—all to no avail. The funny thing is that, after all this searching, I found the right contract manufacturer just ten minutes away from my house. You never know where the help is going to come from.

SERENDIPITY IN A CUP OF COFFEE

It all began with a friendship I struck up at a bakery. I met Pierre Paroz at Panera Bread, of all places, where we were both regulars. I used to get coffee every morning at 7:00 and then sit in the corner and work. Next to me, in the same corner, a White man was there every day before me. A little later, around 8:00 a.m., he would meet with other men. After a couple of weeks, he introduced himself one morning, and we started talking. We instantly hit it off.

That evening, I went to a pumpkin-carving event at my daughter's school. When I walked in with my daughter, Chelsea, there was Pierre, to whom I had just spoken that morning, sitting on the floor and carving a pumpkin with his kid. It turns out his daughter and mine were in the same class. We started a friendship, and eventually, he started mentoring me. He was a businessman and very kind. He was also very family-oriented with strong Christian values, so we were almost like brothers. He even invited me to his church group while he was mentoring me about my business.

One time, I met Pierre at a Starbucks. I was going through a rough patch; I was in between jobs and feeling pretty bad about it. And it was Christmas. I have a family here and I also have a family back home in Ghana that expects me to support them from time to time. Even when I don't have a job, I still have to support them, because the conditions in Ghana are worse than mine here in the States. I was telling Pierre how that Christmas was going to be difficult for us. I wasn't asking him for anything other than a sympathetic ear. We were just talking, and I was telling him how I was feeling.

Pierre got up and said to follow him. Right across from the Starbucks was a bank. He went inside, withdrew some money, put it in an envelope, and handed it to me. I was in shock, but I thanked him and accepted the gift.

When it was time for me to start looking for contract manufacturers, I reached out to my friend and mentor. I said, "Hey, Pierre, I've got a problem. I need some money to be able to scale this business." I thought he might have an idea for how I could fundraise or find a new investor. He asked me what my plan was, and I gave him an overview. He grilled me extensively, and then he said, "Okay, this is what we're going to do. Come to my office. I'm going to set up a meeting so you can meet with me, my CEO, and my CFO. Come and pitch to us. Just tell us what you want us to do for you."

I said, "No problem," but inside I was thinking, *I don't have a pitch.*

In fact, I had a problem pitching: It makes me nervous, and I struggle to get my point across. But I knew I had to do it. Because of my difficulty in pitching, I had joined Toastmasters International to help me with my presentation skills. Sometimes, when I had a big presentation, I'd practice with my Toastmasters group first. I met my good friend Robert Killins, who is now one of the biggest fans of True Shea, at a Toastmasters meeting.

So the following week, I went to American Micro Products and gave my presentation to Pierre and his CEO and CFO. They hadn't had a whole lot of exposure to shea butter until they met me. They are a manufacturing company, and then I came along with my deli container of shea butter and a dream. I knew it was a long shot, because they're an engineering company, not a health and beauty company, but I knew that if anyone could help me scale my business, it would be Pierre.

I did struggle, but I got through my pitch. I explained the product, my plans and retail partnerships, and what I would need from them. They asked questions and took some notes. After they conferred for a few minutes, Pierre smiled and said, "I think we can help each other."

What happened next completely blew me away. From that very day, they took over all my manufacturing and helped me build True Shea. Pierre and his team took a big chance on me. American Micro Products also contributed toward the seed money I needed to get my product ready for Kroger's shelves. Pierre is the current CEO, and Federico COO and CFO of American Micro. The relationship started with Pierre, but Federico continues to spearhead all the investment and growth that has led to True Shea's success. Both of them were very instrumental in the growth of True Shea. And all of this came from a chance encounter at Panera Bread.

With the help of American Micro Products, we figured out how to scale the production. It usually takes a couple of weeks from when the product is shipped to its arrival at the retail store. Since I knew that my local Kroger, Harpers Point, was one of the stores that would be selling the products, I would go to that store a few times a day to check on the shipment. One Friday evening after work, I stopped by and saw my product on the shelf. I screamed with joy so loudly the store clerk standing next to me asked me if I was okay. I told him it was my product—and then we screamed together.

BE OPEN

Your situation might not work out exactly as you think, so be flexible. I've found investors in parking lots. Sometimes you strike up a conversation, and it turns out you can help each other. You never know where opportunity is going to be. If you aren't open, you can miss out.

If I hadn't broadened my search for a manufacturing partner, if I hadn't been open-minded, I wouldn't have had this opportunity. Rather than speaking only with manufacturers who specialized in health and beauty products, I sought out a friend with an engineering company. You have to think outside the box. You can't just reach out to partners already in your niche. In fact, when I went to health and beauty manufacturers, they told me they couldn't mass produce my product. I needed to be open to finding a better solution.

The original recipe of True Shea was not scalable. We had to alter the recipe a little bit in order to make it feasible without breaking the large mixing machines. For the greater good, I had to listen to other ideas from other people and let go of my original recipe; if I hadn't, True Shea would have broken the commercial mixers just like it broke all those cake mixers in my basement. Being open to change is often the only way you can keep moving forward.

7

FUNDING

Funding is a whole new game. Early funding, before you make a profit, comes in two ways: debt and equity. Primarily, debt is taking a loan on credit from a bank. Simply put, equity is trading a piece of the ownership of your business for money. There's always a debate about whether you should go with equity or debt, and I get asked this all the time. They both have trade-offs. It's not an easy answer. One of the difficult decisions is what you give up for the money and under what circumstances you give it up.

If you fund with debt, the bank is typically going to ask you for your collateral, which is your house. If your business doesn't take off and you're not able to pay, they might foreclose on your house to cover the loan repayment. If your business is a success, you'll be able to pay back the loan and will even be eligible for more financing. However, not everybody can qualify for debt, because you need to have a good credit score. If your credit score is not good, you probably won't be able to fund your company with debt.

Investors are not going to take your house, but they will take part of your business. They're going to ask for a piece of your company. If your company fails, your investor will lose their money. You get to keep your house, but the damage to your reputation might mean that you can't get investors again—or that they'll ask for more of your company in exchange for their investment. But if you are a success, you will owe your investors a share of that success. If you make money, they're going to take a piece of it.

At a high level, that's roughly what you have to understand and consider before you proceed with debt or equity funding. What are you willing to risk? Do you want to part with your house if you fail or a piece of your company if you succeed? I went in for a combination of the two options. Early on, I used credit to get my company started, then, when I had built it enough to attract investors, I shifted to equity. Provided you are smart about it—you are able to repay your debt and don't give away too much equity—this is a formula for success.

CREDIT

The secrets to using credit are that you must have a good credit score and you must pay back your loans. Because of my MBA in finance and my banking experience, I knew that my good credit score would give me all kinds of privileges. I was somewhat informed because of my financial savviness, and I knew I'd need to keep my credit score high.

The first part of that was keeping my day job. I always had a job alongside my business, so I always had a high credit score. With a job and a high credit score, the banks are willing to lend. In the very beginning, that meant credit cards. Because of that high credit score, I was able to get a 0 percent interest rate for some credit cards. I was able to pick up fifteen thousand dollars from whatever bank on their Visa card at 0 percent interest rate for twelve or eighteen months.

I used that initial influx of cash to buy products. Within that time period—that twelve or eighteen months of free credit—I'd sell all the products I'd purchased so that I could pay that fifteen thousand dollars back. Being able to borrow money at a 0 percent interest rate was a huge benefit and boost to the early days of my company. But I made sure I paid it all back. Then, because paying it back kept my credit score high—and because I wasn't wasting precious capital on interest—I was able to get another card at 0 percent.

That meant I could now carry thirty thousand dollars on credit cards at 0 percent interest. When the time came, I again paid it all back. I'll say it one more time: Paying off the cards before the interest kicks in is crucial; if you don't have the money to pay it off, your credit score will take a hard hit, and you won't be able to get good rates.

When you start to scale, your need for capital will also scale. You're going to need more than you can get on a credit card. When I began using a manufacturing partner, I needed a significant amount of money. That's when I started approaching the banks. I took out a loan to continue growing the business at this higher level. That's also when I brought in equity investors and gave out a piece of my company.

EQUITY

Once I found a manufacturing partner, I needed money to buy manufacturing inputs and pay for marketing and administrative work, so I started my search for equity funding. Fortunately for me, some of my friends are successful entrepreneurs in Cincinnati, and some were already my mentors. This is where my network literally paid off and mentoring and funding—how to get it and who from—were intertwined.

Steve Hightower

I met Steve Hightower at a Cincinnati Chamber of Commerce event many, many years ago when he was on a panel talking about how to scale your business. Prior to going to the event, I researched him online and noticed he was in the petroleum industry. Armed with this information, I went to the event with him as my target speaker contact. At the time, Ghana had struck oil, so I decided to get his attention with this subject. During the question-and-answer session after his talk, I introduced myself and told him about the oil and gas opportunities in Ghana.

Well, my research paid off. I got his attention with the oil and gas opportunities, and he scheduled a follow-up meeting with me in his office in Middletown. The meeting was scheduled for 10:00 a.m., but fortunately for me, he arrived late, so he asked if we could go to lunch instead. During our time together, I told him about my background, including my MBA in marketing and finance and my experience in financial analysis with various Fortune 500 companies.

He also shared more about his background, including how he started as a janitor and grew his company to a few million dollars in revenue. This man was a straight-up hustler. He taught me my first lesson in hustling. He made me aware that there was a difference between working with Fortune 500 companies and running a small business. He told me that, in the corporate world, things work in a systematic way: You start from A and proceed to Z. In a small business, you start from A, go to G, then to Y, then to E and then to U; you might eventually end up at Z, but the path certainly isn't straightforward. At the time, so early in my career, I didn't really understand, but now I get it, and it was a fantastic insight.

I told him I was trying to do business with Fortune 500 companies, including Cintas and Kroger. Now, Steve does business with General Motors and BP (British Petroleum)—the big players. I believe he was the largest diversity supplier with Kroger at some point, and he knew this space very well. He taught me another lesson in doing business with large corporations. He said it takes an average of two years or more to land a contract with a major retailer. At the time, I thought this was an exaggeration, but I found it to be true—if you are lucky. In the world of hustling, Steve's word is gospel.

Although the oil business did not materialize in Ghana, Steve and I became fast friends and he mentored me in the process. Eventually, he became not only a mentor and a great cheerleader but one of my early investors.

Carl Satterwhite

As I shared earlier, I first met Carl Satterwhite at the Harpers Point Kroger when he was buying chicken for his wife. I had attended an event called "Unpolished" at Crossroads Church a few years earlier, where I heard Carl speak. Unfortunately, I was unable to speak with him that day, but then a few years later, I approached him at that Kroger. I quickly went into my pitch, telling him where I had first heard him and that I was trying to get my shea butter products into Kroger. I also quickly let him know that I knew Steve Hightower, who was my mentor at the time, to give me some credibility. With the combination of Kroger and Steve, I immediately got his attention. When Carl told me he had to go buy that chicken and gave me his business card, I thought to myself, *What a good husband!*

After Carl and I became friends, his company sponsored an event called "Zoophoria" at the Cincinnati Zoo. This was a big event, with an all-you-can-eat buffet, an open bar, and dancing. My wife at the time was excited to go, so I texted Carl for tickets. He texted me back: *Will call.* I thought that meant someone would call me to explain how to get the tickets. As the date approached, my wife asked where the tickets were. So I texted Carl again, and he repeated, *Will call.* So, again, I thought he was going to call me back with the ticket information. On the day of the event, I finally showed my ex-wife the texts, saying I was frustrated that no one had called yet. She laughed and explained that *will call* is an office or a kiosk where you can pick up tickets at the event. I had no idea!

A few years down the road, when I had a purchase order from Kroger and needed to raise money, I reached out to Carl for help. We met at least once a week for many months. He made several phone calls to his ex-P&G buddies for manufacturing assistance, but none of them really worked out. He eventually went on to become one of my very first investors.

Ed Rigaud

Although I had never met Ed Rigaud, Carl Satterwhite often mentioned his name as one the most successful and influential people in Cincinnati. Carl referred to him as the Godfather. *If he calls someone the Godfather*, I thought, *that someone must be pretty important.* So I looked up Ed on Google out of curiosity and began to follow his career.

One day, I was working in my office in Union Hall when I saw someone in the building who looked like Ed Rigaud. (Union Hall, owned and managed by Cintrifuse, is a great co-working space in Cincinnati where startups work from. I made most of my business connections and longtime contacts there. I am sometimes referred to as the mayor of Union Hall.) I went out to double-check, and sure enough, it was him. At the time, he was having a meeting with a few other businessmen, including the CEO of Cintrifuse, Pete Blackshaw, and Dave Foxx. Both grew to become great cheerleaders of True Shea. I promised myself, *No matter what, I am going to talk to Ed.*

I quicky ran into the parking garage and picked up some True Shea samples. I came back to the office and got my laptop. Then, I went and sat in the foyer at the main entrance to the building. I double-checked with the receptionist at the front desk to make sure there was no other door to the building that Ed could leave from, and he said no. So I sat on the couch and waited. I thought, *This man is not leaving this building without talking to me.*

I sat there for about two hours. They were having a long discussion. Finally, I saw him approaching through the door, and I took my stance. Pete walked with the other businessmen to the door and said goodbye, and that's when I made my move. I introduced myself to Ed Rigaud and told him about my shea butter business. Within the same sentence, I made him aware that I was negotiating with Kroger and that Carl Satterwhite and Steve Hightower were my mentors. I knew I had to drop these names to get his attention within the first thirty seconds.

My trick worked, and he gave me his business card so I could follow up with him later. I met with Ed a few times and, in addition to being my mentor, he became my investor. Carl Satterwhite, Ed Rigaud, Steve Hightower, and I continued to meet for years, and I would update them on my developments. They saw me grow from strength to strength, beating one challenge after another. This evolution made them realize that I was in it for the long haul, which is what most investors expect of their investees. Ed is a natural teacher and connector to many of us in the community. He would connect us to people before we even asked.

Jessica Tooley

I ran into Jessica Tooley in the parking lot at a local gym in Cincinnati and talked to her about my business. We became friends, and she joined True Shea as an early investor. In addition to being an investor, Jessica warehouses my products in her house. Although we have space at American Micro Products to warehouse our products, American

Micro Products is far away from my house, and they only work four days a week.

As a traveling hustler and salesman, I have to have products within close proximity at all times. I also still sell products to a few local stores in Cincinnati and pass out samples. In order to meet those supply needs, I have three other smaller warehouses in addition to the AMP warehouse. The first one is my car; the trunk is always packed with products. The second warehouse is at our old house, where my daughter lives with her mom half the time. And the third warehouse is Jessica's house. I prefer Jessica's warehouse because she is a very organized person, so the products are always neatly arranged, while at my old house, I am responsible for arranging the products—a job I don't do very well!

Jessica's funding provides crucial support for our business, but she has also been willing to give up her personal space to help the business grow. That kind of commitment and belief in the business is priceless.

Brad Trucksis

When I was still looking for a contract manufacturer, I knew I'd need to *pay* the contract manufacturer, so I needed to raise additional money. When I initially met Pierre Paroz, he introduced me to Brad Trucksis, who become my friend, mentor, and Christian brother. I met with Brad one evening to try and convince him to invest in my company so I could produce more of my product.

Pierre introduced us at the local Panera Bread where I originally met Pierre. They invited me to a local men's group that met on Friday mornings. This Christian group has helped shape my life. Brad worked for P&G for many years and was very knowledgeable about the skincare industry and shea butter. Brad is one of the very few White men who knew about shea butter before we met.

Brad and I met monthly for several years as he helped me grow my business. When I finally got my order from Kroger, I went to him for financial assistance. Brad is a very meticulous person by virtue of his P&G training. He likes to see things in black and white, so he grilled me several times about how I was going to use his money, and he also asked about my long-term growth strategy.

After a few weeks, I finally convinced him to invest with me. He asked me to meet him at his house around 8:00 p.m., as he was traveling out of the country the next day for two weeks. When I got to his house, he was out feeding his horses, so I had to wait a bit until he was done. He already had written the check, but he wanted to grill me one more time because we were seriously behind schedule to deliver on our first purchase order to Kroger.

He asked, "When do you have to deliver this product?"

I told him in ten days.

"Do you have the shea butter?"

I said no.

"Do you have a contract manufacturer?"

I said no.

He laughed and said, "I am not sure why I am even investing in you. By P&G training, I'm not used to this number of unknowns in a venture. I don't really understand how you are going to get this done, but, somehow, I have faith you." He handed me a check and left for his trip to Europe.

The influx of funding was great for my business, don't get me wrong. But to earn his trust, I had a lot more work to do. Not only was I still looking for a contract manufacturer, but I also had to raise about $250,000 in seed money while ramping up sales and acquiring more raw materials. After many months and lots of hustle, I ended up raising close to that.

In addition to Brad, I approached approximately seventeen other people. Fortunately, I got some more yesses and was able to raise almost all of the seed money in time. This was a huge relief. Once we had the contract manufacturer, we could keep up with production and ship orders out as they came in. To my relief, I was no longer by myself in the basement making shea butter cream.

By the time Brad came back, we had produced the product and delivered it to Kroger. His trust in me during a difficult situation allowed us both to realize a good result.

The combination of both loans and equity—the flexibility it gave me—was a good way to go for my business. If you have debt, you're paying interest rates, and it takes away cash flow from the business. And if your credit score is low, you're probably not going to get any loans from a bank, so that's you shooting your own foot. If your funding is equity, you don't have to pay it right now, and this will allow your money to grow, but you will owe some of your winnings later to your investors. It's important to choose wisely and make the best choice for your own situation, but a combination of both, if you can arrange it, is often the best way to go.

8

MAKING YOUR COMPANY VISIBLE

One of the expected challenges every business faces is brand awareness. The challenge is more difficult for small and medium-size enterprises and for diverse-owned businesses because of the lack of funds for advertisements. I went through a lot of trouble to get onto Kroger shelves, and then Walmart, only to find ourselves face to face with lack of brand awareness problems. We were on so many shelves, and no one knew who we were!

True Shea was on the shelves at Kroger and Walmart with all the other brand names: Olay body lotion, Vaseline, Gold Bond, CeraVe, Eucerin, Aquaphor, Jergens, Nivea, and Dove, among others. True Shea has one facing—one jar of shea butter cream visible on the shelf, with other jars stacked behind—while these other brands have about ten to twenty-five facings. These are huge brands that dwarf a small operation like ours, and with so many of their products on the shelves it was hard to notice ours. The story was the same in all the major stores. Brand names spend billions of dollars on ads; True Shea did not even have a marketing budget. The significant amount of dollars spent by big brands provides them brand awareness, making them more recognizable on the shelves to consumers.

Most customers already know what they want; they go directly to the right aisle and grab it. Most people are in a hurry between their busy jobs and taking children to school and extra-curriculars. They are in the store shopping with three or four kids and are probably also on their cell phone. As a result, nobody is really spending the time to notice a new no-name brand on the shelf.

This situation resulted in less-than-expected sales performance for us. We were in fifteen hundred stores with little sales revenues, but we somehow made enough to stay there. We have been in the stores for four years now. Most new small and diversity brands that get onto the retail shelf in stores across the country are usually discontinued in less than six months. This is not a problem isolated to Kroger.

Now, don't get me wrong: I am very grateful for the opportunity, but it can be a difficult uphill climb for a small and diversity business to make a product visible to the customer. We continue to try any option we can find.

SOCIAL MEDIA

In today's social media age, we tried to use social media to direct traffic from social media platforms into the stores to purchase our products. But there's a disconnect between the online customer and the in-store customer. In-store customers are usually older and prefer to shop in person. Online customers swear by the internet and prefer to shop online, and they are typically of the younger generations.

So, when we started doing a social media campaign to drive customers to the store, it didn't really work. When a customer saw an ad on social media, they wanted to buy the product right away. It didn't make too much sense to leave their homes to go and look for the product in Kroger. Even when they eventually went to Kroger to shop, they forgot about the True Shea ad they saw six weeks earlier. Kroger offers yellow tag sales and digital coupons, which we used, but it only helped so far.

THIS BOOK

After identifying our number-one problem to be brand awareness, I continued to look for a solution. During the previous year, I had been invited to tell my story at more than fifty events. I regularly got a lot of applause after I spoke. I had also been reading about how to build a brand. I stumbled over an article that talked about Uncle Nearest Whiskey. This brand had used storytelling to promote its products and had sold $100 million in the first five years. Based on these two factors—the apparent interest in my story and the obvious success of using storytelling to sell a product—I decided to follow Uncle Nearest's example and use storytelling to promote True Shea. I decided the best way was to tell this story and sell the resulting book in Kroger stores, where we already had plenty of distribution.

About six months after conceiving this idea, I was fortunate to meet Fawn Weaver, the founder and CEO of Uncle Nearest, at Xavier University Cintas Center, where she had been invited as a guest speaker at the Women in Business & Leadership luncheon. Coincidentally, she was speaking on the very stage where I pre-launched my book a month before. I thought this would be an opportunity to test my hypothesis about telling my story, and so I asked her to what degree she thought storytelling was helpful in selling a product. She answered 100 percent. I shared some shea butter samples with her and have kept in touch to this day.

Manny with his role model, Fawn Weaver,
founder and CEO of Uncle Nearest

I took this bold idea and shared it with my mentor-in-chief, Angel Colon, the supplier diversity director at Kroger at the time. I explained the following advantages to him:

- Selling the book in stores would generate sales for Kroger and True Shea and would even drive sales of the product itself.

- I could tour Kroger stores across the country, signing books to create awareness of the book and our products.

- I would give out free samples of our cream to create awareness and direct customers to the specific aisle to buy the products.

Angel immediately made the connection between the book sales and the promotion of the products and liked the idea very much. His immediate concern was how Kroger would take to the idea of someone putting their name on a book to be sold in their stores. How would the legal department respond? How about public relations? They would probably want to read every word in the book. At this point, I left it with him. He said he would get back to me.

Surprisingly, the approval from Kroger to go ahead with the book was not as painful a process as I thought. They must have liked the idea, or else Angel was extremely persuasive. A few days later, Angel told me he had gotten permission from legal and introduced me to the director of public relations to make my case. She walked me though the things I needed to know and also gave me the go-ahead for the book, and then it was time to meet the category manager for books. It was crucial to get him on board, since he'd be in charge of getting my book into stores.

Around this time, I went to a National Minority Supplier Development Council conference. The first night of the event, I was in my hotel running on the treadmill when I got a call from Angel. I thought, *I better pick up this call*, and I got off the treadmill. Angel told me he was leaving Kroger, and although he really enjoyed his work, it was time to pursue another opportunity. He also promised he would make sure I met with the books category manager before he left.

True to his word, a week later, he set up a meeting with the books category manager, but unfortunately his daughter got sick that day so we had to reschedule. Now Angel had less than a week left with the company. He finally got me a meeting with the category manager two days before he left Kroger. This was a gesture I truly appreciated and respected.

When Angel told the books category manager about the book, he was on board. Our plan was to launch the book in February 2022 for two reasons. First, it was to celebrate Black History Month, and second, February is our biggest selling month to promote True Shea. But due to many obstacles, February rolled by, and the book was not ready.

EVENTS AND AWARDS

Anything that makes your product visible can get it into the hands of your customers. That includes more than just the shelf or online shopping. Especially when you're selling to local stores or in a regional market, local events, outreach, and awards can help people become aware of you.

In 2020, Carl Satterwhite invited me to sit at his table at a Martin Luther King Jr. celebration. This well-organized event was sponsored by Kroger. During the event, I ran into Angel, who offered to introduce me to the CEO of Kroger. But before the introduction, he asked me, "Do you have any shea butter samples with you?" Now, in the early days of the business, I never left the house without shea butter samples in my pocket.

I responded, "I definitely have some samples."

I quickly grabbed them and followed him. He walked me over to the CEO and introduced me as one of the rising vendors for Kroger. He also shared with him that we were giving back to Ghana by creating jobs and building water wells.

About four years after this event, I was invited to the NAACP Freedom Fund Dinner in Cincinnati by the vice mayor of Cincinnati, Jan-Michele Kearney, one the biggest supporters of True Shea. At this event, I was again introduced to the CEO of Kroger, Rodney McMullen, this time by the new supplier diversity director. Fortunately, McMullen remembered me from the previous meeting.

Our second order for additional stores should have happened in 2020 but was postponed because of COVID-19. During this period, business was slow, because we were primarily in brick-and-mortar stores, with very little online presence. I decided to make good use of my time by donating shea butter samples to frontline workers. If you remember, during COVID-19, we were all advised to regularly wash our hands and use hand sanitizers. These two very helpful acts, although good for curbing the spread of COVID, led to dry hands. Our shea butter is very highly concentrated, making it a great moisturizer. I went around to the Kroger stores in Cincinnati and donated True Shea samples to the employees. They gave me permission to go into the break rooms and give the samples out to the workers on their lunch break. In some stores, I gave them to the store managers to share with employees.

Pre-Book Launch

Even though my book wasn't ready, I still wanted to do something for Black History Month in 2022. A friend suggested we get a box made that looked like a book and put samples of our product in it. We could then have a very early launch party for the book—a pre-book launch party. My marketing team designed the book box with the product samples in it, and they also included information about the upcoming book. People could read about our product and the book, and when they opened the box, they could experience the product.

The pre-book launch was a very last-minute idea we came up with over the Christmas break. As a result, it was hurriedly put together. The first thing I needed for this event was money, so I contacted the new supplier diversity manager. I met with her and told her about the pre-book launch and its benefits for True Shea and Kroger. She asked me how much I needed, and I asked her how much she could afford. At this time, I was really running behind. The event was only a few weeks away, so I got straight to the point. We agreed on an amount in less than five minutes and were able to keep things moving. She came through with this request so fast that I said, "Hmm. She's good. This may be another Angel."

Speaking of Angel, at the time of the pre-book launch, he was no longer working with Kroger. However, since he had been such an integral part of my journey and knew my story better than anyone

Angel Colon speaking at Manny's pre-book launch at Xavier University's Cintas Center.

else, we decided to invite him to speak. He gratefully agreed to come and speak at the event.

About a week before the launch, we only had twenty people registered. This led to my event planner getting real with me and letting me have it, because I had planned for too many attendees. To ease this tension, we decided that I would be responsible for filling the room, and the rest of the team would be in charge of marketing and event coordination. That way, I could get them off my case and try and do some selling. Now, I am a very last-minute person, but even I thought I may have pushed this too far. The very last week before the event, I started making phone calls, trying to get people to attend. Eventually, I found a few more bodies to fill the space; I believe we may have had about 150 people attend.

It was a very colorful event, complete with African drumming and dancing. The event was well attended by former and current Kroger associates, including my greatest cheerleaders: supplier diversity manager, category manager, and supplier diversity director. The highlight of the event for me was when the vice mayor of Cincinnati, Jan-Michele Kearney, walked in and was asked to say a few words. On the stage, she took out an empty jar of True Shea she had just finished using. She said some very nice things about me and about the company, but that gesture was striking. Later that week, I started getting pictures of empty jars from other True Shea customers.

The week after the pre-book launch, I was walking down the street next to Kroger headquarters when I heard somebody honking at me. When I turned around, it was the vice mayor waving at me and shouting congratulations on the event.

A year later, for Black History Month 2023, the Kroger supplier diversity team recommended I be featured in the Kroger events calendar. As a result of this, the senior creative director of Kroger came from Portland, Oregon, to Cincinnati to take pictures and shoot videos of me and the business. We started with taking pictures in one store and then went to a studio to make a video. I was asked about my days in Tansia, when I witnessed six-year-old kids carrying water on their heads before going to school. After a while, I broke down in tears. Tears ran down my face and messed up my makeup, so the interview process was paused for me to regroup and have my makeup redone.

In 2020, Kroger nominated me for the Supplier of the Year category of the Ohio Minority Supplier Development Council Awards, and I won it. This was during COVID-19, so the event was online, with very few ways to celebrate. When I again won an OMSDC award, this time for Emerging Business of the Year in 2022, the awards event was in-person in Cleveland. I was fortunate to have been invited to sit at the Kroger table and get to share the moment with the team that made all this happen.

In July 2023, Kroger invited me to speak at their Bring Your Child to Work Day. I had just returned from a three-week trip to Ghana,

Stephanie Burton, Manny, and Angel Colon (left to right) at the Ohio Minority Supplier Development Council Gala, where True Shea was awarded the Emerging Business of the Year.

where I had recently been made a chief of a local village (more on this later), and I brought along quite a few pictures of the ceremony and my visit. There were eight groups of kids, with ten kids in each group, who came to my presentation. I shared my journey from Ghana to the United States, talked about the challenges I went through, and showed pictures of my visit. I also shared samples of unscented shea butter products with them, so they could feel and smell it in its natural form. Now, shea butter itself has a unique smell to it. One of the kids smelled the shea butter and said, "This smells like Africa," and we all started laughing. This kid had never been to Africa, and I am still wondering what he meant by that, but I loved his enthusiasm.

In October 2023, I was invited to the NAACP Freedom Fund Dinner by Jan-Michele Kearney, vice mayor of Cincinnati. The purpose of the dinner was to honor distinguished members of Cincinnati society. The speaker at this event was Rep. Hakeem Jeffries, minority leader of the U.S. House of Representatives, who gave a great speech about how to bind together to produce a truly color-blind America. The annual Cincinnati NAACP Freedom Fund Dinner is a long-standing tradition that brings together NAACP members and community supporters to raise funds to support its operations. Cincinnati NAACP has been working diligently since 1915 to eliminate discrimination and inequality in fifty-two neighborhoods and in the communities surrounding Cincinnati.

Getting your product on store shelves—even in one thousand stores, is only the first step of a long journey. Okay, maybe it's the thousandth step on an even longer journey, but my point is that the job is not done. You still have work left to do. To make sure your customers know who you are and to find new customers who trust your product, you must make yourself visible. That means marketing, yes, but it also means going out into the community, participating with your partners and the people, and—most of all—giving back.

In 2023, our sales were not exactly where we needed them to be in order for us to be profitable, and I was getting concerned. I reached out to Kroger's chief marketing officer and his team members, as well as to the merchandising group and the vice president of merchandising, for a solution to my problem. They encouraged me to have a meeting with all the parties involved, including my category managers and brokers, to find a lasting solution to grow True Shea within Kroger. We had this meeting a few weeks later and this was the turning point of my business, which led to an increase in my sales.

PART 3

GIVING BACK

One of my major goals in starting a company was giving back. I wanted to continue to be a part of the social insurance I had known back in Ghana. But it can be difficult for a small company to find a way to help. I wondered, *How can I contribute without breaking the bank?* I didn't have the money to simply write a check like the big companies could. But I had products people could use, and I had a partner in Kroger who had given me so many opportunities.

When COVID-19 hit, Kroger was the obvious place to start. Shea butter is a great moisturizer, and because we all had to wash our hands constantly during the pandemic, a good moisturizer was crucial for everyone. The more you wash your hands and the more hand sanitizer you use, the drier your hands become. Giving out samples of True Shea to Kroger employees began as a small way to return the support the company had given me.

Then I reached out to Cincinnati Children's Hospital to do the same. I went to Mercy Health Hospital with samples as well. We gave shea butter to all the frontline workers to moisturize the hands that had helped so many people.

Around the same time, I was invited by the University of Cincinnati to be among the vendors giving out free products to welcome African American and other diversity freshmen. My daughter and I set up a table and handed out samples for an hour or so. Just before I was getting ready to leave, a young lady walked up to me and asked, "Are you the owner of True Shea?"

I said I was, and she continued, "My mother has cancer, and the only thing that works for her is True Shea. I'm forming a nonprofit organization to give products to cancer patients. Would you mind donating some of your products?" Of course I didn't mind. I arranged to get her a supply of samples.

Making connections with people and embracing opportunities when they arise paid off again. We have been able to make small contributions to many institutions now. Giving out samples of your product is a great way to start, but if you want to make a larger impact—as I do—you have to think bigger. Once you start making money, you can funnel some of it into meaningful programs to help people. In my case, that meant investing in our local communities—both in Cincinnati and in Ghana. All the connections you have built to this point can also become crucial partners in doing good.

9

GIVING BACK TO THE UNITED STATES

I t is important for me to give back to my adopted home of Cincinnati, and to the United States in a wider sense. But it is a crucial part of my dream that I connect my new home with my homeland. I want to connect the people and businesses of Africa with those in the United States, and a huge part of that is helping immigrants start their own businesses. As always, this is about building connections and participating in a supportive community.

THE AFRICA AMERICAN TRADE AND INVESTMENT SUMMIT

In addition to being the founder and CEO of Natural Shea Care, I am also the founding CEO of Africa America Business Promotion (AABP). I founded AABP to promote business between Africa and the United States. In this capacity, I organized the first Africa American Trade and Investment Summit at the Cincinnati Chamber of Commerce in 2019.

This event had attendees from Ghana, Canada, China, and the United States. The summit was sponsored by Hightower Petroleum; its CEO, Steve Hightower, is a longtime mentor of mine and was a speaker at the event as well. Cintas Corporation, also a sponsor, was fully represented by Phillip Holloman, the company's then president; Pamela Coleman, then director of supplier diversity; John Vu, VP of sourcing; and Tom Schlau, then senior director of strategic sourcing. The RCF Group was represented by its president, Carl Satterwhite, my mentor and coach. The welcoming speaker was Jill Meyer, president of the Cincinnati Chamber of Commerce. The keynote speaker was the Honorable Alan Kyerematen, Ghana's minister of trade and former ambassador to the United States. Other attendees included representatives from Kroger, Procter & Gamble, the Cincinnati Chamber of Commerce, and the Ohio Minority Supply Development Council.

At the summit, I brokered a meeting between Ghana's minister of trade and the Cintas team, led by Phillip Holloman. This meeting subsequently led to sourcing opportunities between Ghana and Cintas Corporation.

Together with our partners, AABP and NSC have sourced more than $10 million worth of products from Ghana into the United States under the African Growth and Opportunity Act. We are also working to establish the Africa Water Project. With this project, we will source a product from an African country, sell it into the U.S., and then use a portion of the sales to build a water well in the country where the product is sourced. We built and donated a water well in Ghana in collaboration with Kroger in February 2022, and we have plans for more.

PODCAST WITH BLUE ALLIANCE

I appeared on a podcast with Blue Alliance, called *Between US*, and discussed the following topics:

- Being an entrepreneur and a consummate networker:
  I love people!

- Community is powerful: connecting me to my next step

- Being an immigrant living and working in this country

- How having an accent has given me markers for awareness
  and teachable moments

- Building wells in Ghana

- True Shea and other venture adventures

- How reaching out to the CEO of Cintas Corporation
  when I was a student at Xavier University jump-started
  my first business

- This book you are currently reading

IDEA SUMMIT IN 2022

The Northern Kentucky Chamber of Commerce and St. Elizabeth Healthcare partnered with another organization in the region to host the first IDEA Summit, titled "Building an Inclusive Community: The Business Case for Diversity, Equity, and Inclusion." The event was held on Friday, June 10, at the St. Elizabeth Training and Education Center and addressed removing barriers to employment, effective talent attraction and retention strategies, the importance of an inclusive workplace culture, and building a plan for supplier diversity.

At this summit, in conjunction with Angel Colon, the supplier diversity director at Kroger at the time, I shared my story to help diversity and small business owners get their products into Kroger and other retailers. We also discussed how to scale their business in general. A gentleman from the audience approached me and said my story was very inspiring and invited me to his home for dinner to serve as an inspiration to his sons.

THE ECONOMIC COMMUNITY AND DEVELOPMENT INSTITUTE

I worked at the Economic & Community Development Institute (ECDI) from 2018 to 2023 as a relationship manager. ECDI is fiercely dedicated to ensuring that every entrepreneur—regardless of where they came from, where they live, their gender, or their race—has access to funding and business mentoring services. I really enjoyed working with ECDI because of their dedication to helping diverse groups, women, and—more importantly—immigrants. As an immigrant who formed my own company, I wish I had known about the services they provide, because they are very helpful to small businesses.

I also especially enjoyed the opportunity ECDI provided me to serve immigrants, particularly those from Africa. Immigrants can be very skeptical of the system and reluctant to share financial and immigration status with people they don't know. Sometimes they fear being deported. I found that my African clients felt a little more confident in sharing with me, especially the ones who were not yet U.S. citizens. I would sometimes hear them on the phone asking to talk with the African (that's me!). ECDI also has a refugee program that helps refugees get ahead in business. These are all very valuable services that ECDI provides.

As a relationship manager, I was responsible for generating loans, which required working with the client to submit a complete loan package and meeting all the necessary requirements. This role also gave me insight into the process of underwriting a loan. This knowledge came in very handy when it was time to apply for loans for my own company. I was able to submit a complete application backed by all the necessary information, a business plan, and the financial projections needed to easily secure a loan from banks. The steps leading up to forming one's own business are valuable lessons and skills.

MORTAR

In late 2022, I was approached by Procter & Gamble and Kroger to speak at MORTAR, a business development service in Cincinnati. MORTAR's Entrepreneurship Academy helps young entrepreneurs grow their businesses. I spoke to the students about how to scale their business. It was a two-hour session with fifteen or twenty students in a business incubator. This was just another way to give back to the community, to help others who were just starting out get a good start on their careers. As I grew in knowledge and experience, I was able to share with other communities.

10

GIVING BACK TO AFRICA

Kroger, Walmart, Target, and Amazon continue to sell our products, helping to create additional opportunities for economic growth in Africa. I've always been of the belief that it is important to give back. I am very blessed to have been on the receiving end of kindness and I am so grateful to have the opportunity to pay it forward today.

PRODUCING GOOD

Natural Shea Care's products, including True Shea, are manufactured in the United States, but we get most of our raw shea butter from Ghana and make the finished product in Cincinnati. Our work creates economic opportunities in Ghana. When we reach our next benchmark in sales, we will be able to create another manufacturing plant in Ghana to expand production in that country.

During a trip to Ghana, Manny was able to explore the countryside and share his product with the villages he visited.

True Shea sources the raw shea from the shea nut tree in Ghana villages, like the one pictured here, allowing Manny to connect with and give back to the local communities.

We source most of our raw shea butter from a village called Gnani and a city called Tamale. This is a way for me to use my business to give back to the socially and economically disadvantaged women in the Gnani community. NSC pays above-market prices to these women as part of our fair-trade commitment. A portion of our sales is donated to the NSC Community Development Fund to improve working conditions for the people of Ghana by creating schools, constructing much-needed manufacturing facilities, and providing clean drinking water.

The largest portion of our shea comes from Tamale, but we also source from the village of Gnani. Gnani is about four hour's travel from Tamale. It's a little bit of a logistical challenge, and it costs more than producing all of our product in Tamale, but we wanted to offer opportunities to Gnani that wouldn't be available otherwise. We donate a portion of all sales revenues to build water wells in this community. We also provide employment for twenty-five women in the village.

During the Kparigu Yelbu ceremony, the village shows support by wearing their True Shea T-shirts.

Manny and a staff member of Homemade Shea Butter examine shea nuts ahead of the production process in which the nuts are ground to release the fat and oil that is used in True Shea.

Manny likes to be involved in every step of the product creation process and doesn't shy away from hard work. Here, he is grinding shea nuts for True Shea.

Manny and the group leader of Homemade Shea Butter mix the ingredients for True Shea in a large mixing bowl. He involves the whole village to demonstrate how he creates his product.

The process of creating shea butter involves hard work to grind the nuts, release the needed fat and oil, and whip the mixture into a creamy consistency that becomes the True Shea product.

The women of the village forage for nuts and bring them into the village. Then they boil them, process the raw shea into butter, and scoop it. Right now, they all work out in the open. My sister Christie (the one who lives in New Jersey) is in charge of this project. She's trying to build a processing center so the women can work safely and produce premium shea butter. We are currently applying for a grant from the U.S. government to make some sort of improvement.

THE AFRICA WATER PROJECT

During my national service in that very remote village of Tansia, I experienced firsthand the water challenges in this region. Children as young as six years old walked about four miles every morning to fetch water for their families, carrying full pots of water on their heads on their return trip. This would leave them pretty tired before going to school. This made an impression on me, and, when I left this village after a year of teaching, I made a promise to help with the water situation in the region if I made it to the United States. After nearly twenty years in the United States, I was finally able to give back to this region of Africa. In 2022, with the collaboration and generosity of Kroger, I was able to install a clean drinking water well, which is a valuable resource for all the people of Africa, not just Ghana. It was incredible for me to experience this dream finally coming true.

Gnani is a village in the Yendi Municipality of the Northern Region of Ghana, noted mainly for the presence of an alleged witch camp situated in the middle of the town. The village is a multi-tribal community of approximately thirteen thousand people. Their main occupation is crop and fish farming. The community has other resources, including both public and private schools up to junior high. Gnani also has a health center that offers services to more than four thousand people through on-site and outreach programs.

Manny helps a local child carry fresh water to the village for use in homes and daily tasks.

In January 2020, during the pandemic, the spiritual leader of Gnani-Tindang, a multicultural, indigenous settlement within the Gnani community, reached out to individuals and organizations to help in the provision of some basic amenities, such as water, sanitation, and skill development facilities, to improve the living conditions of his people.

This part of the village is also home to more than two hundred people hailing from various villages in northern Ghana who have been accused of witchcraft and banished from their communities. They've been relegated to that village because society looks down on them.

African society, like many others, rejects people who are different in ways they don't understand. They begin to look for other ways of explaining it. For example, if a woman has facial hair, if she grows a beard, she is considered a witch because they can't explain why this happened. If a woman has a mental illness, and the local people don't understand her behavior, they will call her a witch. These women are sent from their homes, often after being abused.

Gnani was the first village to receive a well. My sister Dr. Christie Agawu is in charge of Africa Water Project's Ghana operations, whereas I handle the U.S. operations. She chose this village because it contains more than one hundred ostracized women who were struggling to get water—a precious resource needed for survival. The Gnani well was a collaboration between NSC and Kroger to provide a mechanized borehole, a ten-thousand-liter tank, and five stand pipes for the people

In addition to providing the villages of Ghana with a source of income through purchasing raw shea, Manny, True Shea, and Kroger also give back to the community in other ways. Here, his generosity helped to build a water well in Gnani.

of Gnani-Tindang. This water well saves the women and children from walking five miles to fetch water.

But Gnani is only the first; I hope to install our next water well in Tansia. It will be an amazing opportunity for the people of Tansia, and I am grateful to be able to pay my good fortune forward to help the good people in this remote village. It has been thirty years since I have been in Tansia, and I am looking forward to visiting old friends and making new ones. Because they will have this basic necessity, the children in this village will have more opportunity, more time to study. They can get to school on time and be less tired. And maybe all that starts with a glass of fresh water right from the well.

My dream is continuing to grow, as all dreams should. Clean drinking water is not just a Ghana problem. It is an Africa problem. These wells in northern Ghana are just the beginning. With continued success, NSC will provide fresh drinking water to the people of Africa, one well at a time.

As the Africa Water Project continues to grow, our plan is to go into neighboring countries, such as the Côte d'Ivoire. This country has a lot of cashews. Our plan is to source cashews from Côte d'Ivoire, just like we did in Ghana with the shea butter, to provide economic opportunity in this country by bringing the harvested nuts to the United States to sell to retailers such as Kroger and Walmart. In turn, we will take a portion of that money and build a fresh drinking water well in Côte d'Ivoire.

We will continue to help expand Africa's economy by harvesting natural resources from other areas of Africa. Say another African country has an abundance of avocados. We will create an economic opportunity for the people in that community to harvest the avocados for us to ship to the United States and sell in stores such as Target and Walmart. This, in turn, will help fund additional wells for the good people of Africa.

AN HONOR AND A RESPONSIBILITY

In June 2023, I decided to visit Gnani in person, to familiarize myself with the community and understand their needs. I also visited the water well and spent some time making shea butter with the women who work so hard to produce it for us. While I was there, the village leadership bestowed a very special honor on me.

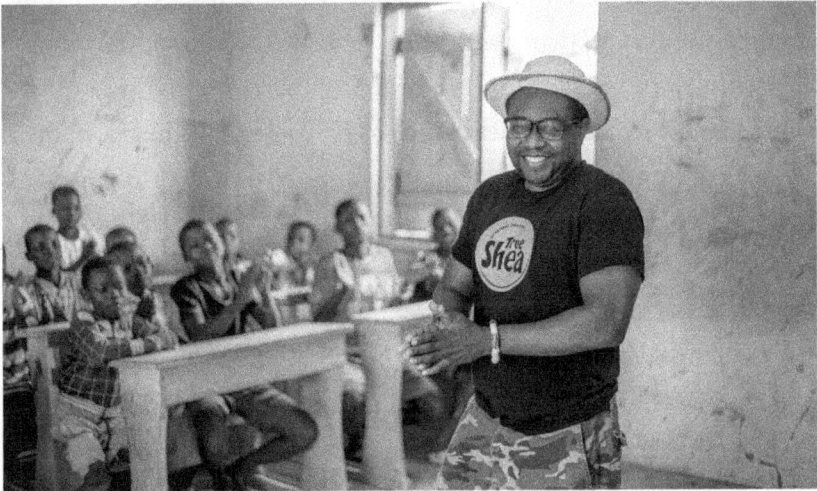

Manny visits a school in Gnani to learn about the conditions and what help is needed.

Our local office arranged transportation to Gnani, and the a photographer, a videographer, one of our operation managers, and I traveled two hours to the village. When we arrived, we drove into the village center. We were in a pickup truck, and the villagers typically don't see vehicles like that. They don't even see people entering their village very often. All the kids in the village came running toward us. Some were shirtless; some didn't have any pants on. And the first words out of their mouth were: "Can we get a soccer ball?"

There were no soccer balls in the whole village. As a kid that played soccer every day growing up, I was really touched by this request. I know how important having access to sports can be, and soccer is a universally loved sport outside the United States. Soccer saved my life. It kept me from getting into trouble, because when you're playing soccer from morning to night, you don't go looking for mischief. I don't know what would've happened to me without it.

So that night, we rushed back to the city before the shops closed. I brought them soccer balls the very next day. At first, we bought only two, but when we handed them to the kids, the chief also wanted a

The kids in Gnani appreciate the wisdom and fun experiences that Manny brings when he comes to visit.

soccer ball, and then each of the adults wanted a soccer ball. Everyone wanted to play. My team and I eventually went back and bought six more soccer balls for the village.

After being swarmed by these future World Cup champions, I needed to present myself to the local chief. This is the most respectful thing to do immediately when you visit a village. Some of the adults asked us to sit outside, and they went in to announce our presence to the chief. They said we were the ones who had funded the well and the shea butter production. We had to take off our shoes, and then we were called in to meet with the chief and the elders.

We met with the spiritual chief of Gnani-Tindang, Tindang-Naa Alhassan Shei. Right off the bat, he said, "Mr. Manny Addo, in collaboration with my subchiefs and other community opinion leaders, I would like to confer upon you the chieftaincy title of Maligu-Naa, development chief."

This was a complete surprise to me, the last thing I would have expected. We had done a lot of work in that village. It's where the first well was built. But I did not expect to be embraced into the village leadership.

The chieftaincy institution has existed since before Ghanaian independence. Before the arrival of White colonialists, chiefs were the administrators of towns, villages, or ethnic groups. The colonial governors originally governed through the heads of clans, families, and chiefs and gradually set up administrative systems with the chiefs as representatives of the people. Modern-day chiefs have their own traditional systems of governance through a hierarchical system running top-down from royalty to subject. This system is now regulated by laws and the constitution, binding activities, and actions that include installations, enstoolments, and enskinments of chiefs. The amended Chieftaincy Act of 2008 officially categorized chiefs into kings, paramountcy and divisional chiefs, subchiefs, and other lower-level chiefs who support the running of the customary and traditional systems. The act also fine-tuned the institutionalization of other legal bodies, such as the National and Regional Houses of Chiefs.

In northern Ghana, spiritual leaders were also classified under the chieftaincy institution, but after the independence of 1957, their authority under the new constitution was taken over by the chiefs, even though in some areas of northern Ghana, the spiritual chiefs—known as the *Tindana*, which literally means "owner of the land"—still held their authority and have allodial land rights and are responsible for the spiritual well-being of the land under their jurisdiction.

The Gnani-Tindang exists under the chief of Gnani, who reports directly to the paramountcy in Yendi of the Northern Region of Ghana. The Tindang also has subchiefs who support him in the day-to-day running of his jurisdiction. One such subchief is the *Maligu-Naa* (development chief). These positions are often given to people who

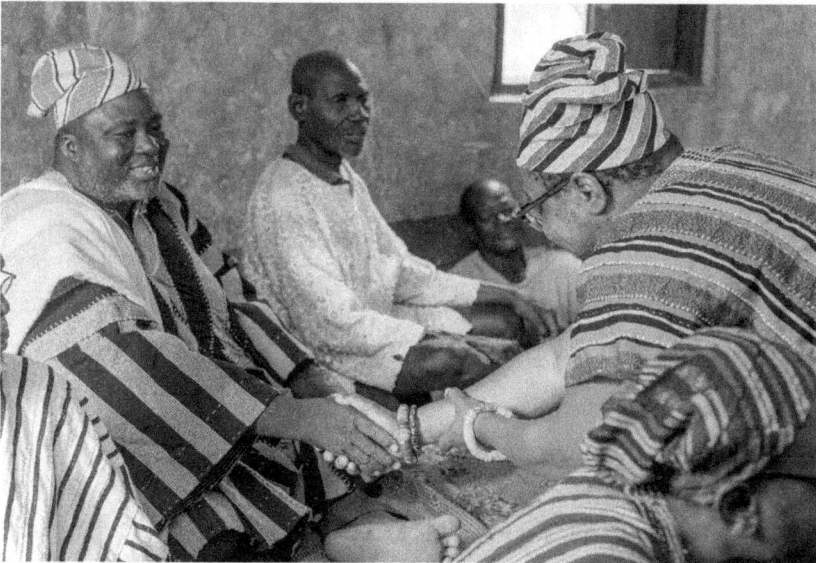

The leaders in Gnani were so grateful for all the contributions Manny has made to their community that they named him a chief of the village. A traditional ceremony took place to celebrate this great honor.

Manny was named as a chief of Gnani during a chieftancy ceremony to thank him for his contributions to the village. Traditional attire is worn to celebrate this great honor.

have exhibited the capacity to respond to the welfare and social needs of the people of the area. The role includes ensuring a peaceful environment for development, mobilizing resources, and attracting investment into the area. The development chief is more or less an ambassador of goodwill for the chief and the people of Gnani-Tindang. It is expected, however, that his activities will not be limited only to the people of Gnani-Tindang but to all the people of Gnani.

I was surprised, but of course I accepted. This was a big honor. With twenty or thirty people in the meeting hall, I knelt down, and the chief blessed me. The chief danced around me, performing an ancient ceremony, and he gave me a cola nut to chew. After that, we left the room with the chief and encountered a group of women drumming and dancing, and I danced with them as well.

They made me development chief of the village on the very first day of my visit. I was there for three days, and my work began immediately. The chief asked me to go and visit the women in the camp so I could see their situation for myself. So I visited them and gave them money. I met a woman who was about eighty or ninety years old. She couldn't see, but she could hear. She hadn't had any medical attention in years. She was sleeping on the floor in a mud hut. The temperature in the hut was about 120 degrees. In spite of such poor circumstances, I was very much impressed at the joy she carried and the way she welcomed me.

This visit left me very depressed, as this woman and others like her live in deplorable conditions. I started tearing up, then just breaking down. It was horrible. This woman had lived such a hard life, but it was now part of my job as a chief to help her. It was now my responsibility to bring economic development to the village, to raise funds, and to help improve these people's conditions. It was a call to action for me.

A couple of things went through my mind. I thought about what a privilege, what an honor, it was to be a chief appointed to serve these people. But with every honor comes responsibility. We'd been doing a lot of work there already, so it was not new, but now it was official. I would be held responsible for community development work in the village.

The chief said there were many elderly women like the one I had met who basically couldn't take care of themselves. These women lived in very poor conditions and were scattered in various parts of the village, making it very difficult to take care of them. The chief made a passionate appeal to me as the new chief of community development to construct an elderly people's home for these women so they could be housed in one area and more easily taken care of.

The chief asked for two things: a soccer ball and an elderly home. The first one was easy. Now I had to work hard to give him his second wish, so one of my next goals is raising money and resources from the United States to be able to build that facility. I plan to honor this obligation, but I also plan to build a school for the children of Gnani as we continue to grow a relationship with them. We also plan to form a soccer club there.

We also plan to build our next well in Tansia, in the village where I performed my national service, because that's where it all started for me, and I want to go back to thank them. I tried to visit during my trip to Gnani, but there was civil unrest in the region. I wonder how many of the people I knew will still be alive. Even without the unrest, it's been almost thirty years, and people don't live too long in that part of the world. I may go next year, if the region calms down by then. We want to build that well when we can.

GETTING THE WORD OUT

Giving back to community is a core part of what I want to do with my business. We donate a portion of sales toward these and other community development projects and will continue to do so. Because of the remoteness of these villages, the cost to build the wells can be quite high. We believe the social impact is high enough to justify the cost, but it can be difficult for a small business like ours to find enough funding. Kroger has been an irreplaceable partner in these endeavors.

Our need to operate profitably while also donating a portion of our sales can be a difficult concept to convey to customers. It can be a struggle to pass on the good work we are doing to the consumer, letting them know they are giving back by purchasing a product. If we ask the consumer to pay a little more, they push back, but if they understand the story, maybe they'd be willing to shoulder a small portion of the cost. And because the jar is so small, it is hard to tell the whole story on the label. It's a bit of a conundrum: We want to be profitable, but we also want to help our community. I have investors who are looking for me to pay back their money (a return on their investment). That's where a project like this book can offer more. It can generate some publicity and even money to help continue these programs.

This all ties back to my dream of coming to the United States and creating international connections through business. Whatever your dream is, it will be challenging. The journey may take longer than you initially think. But with perseverance and the support of cheerleaders, mentors, and partners, you can overcome the obstacles and succeed. Anything is possible if you're willing to do the work.

Now that you've seen how I made my dream come true, it's time for yours to come true. But first, you have to figure out what kind of business you want to build. That's a very powerful decision. I'm asking you to reflect on what you know and what you can do. What is your gift to the world? This question applies not just to business but to any challenge in life.

What is your shea butter?

ACKNOWLEDGMENTS

As I already mentioned in the book, I'm so grateful for the support of Pierre Paroz, Federico Veneziano, Dave Foxx, Carl Satterwhite, Steve Hightower, Jessica Tooley, Ed Rigaud, Brad Trucksis, Vice Mayor Jan-Michele Kearney, Congressman Greg Landsman, Jen Bush, Father Richard Bollman, Angel Colon, Kevin Bein, Scott Farmer, President John Mahama, Dr. Abdul-Nashiru Issahaku, Oluranti Doherty, Sebastian Ashong-Katai, Bryan Whitaker, Dr. Christie Agawu, and Robert Killins.

To my family, Chelsea Addo and Molly Addo, for all the love, support, and encouragement over the years. I really appreciate it.

I also want to thank the following people and organizations:

Special thanks to The Kroger Co. teams for their continued support.

At Union Hall: Maurice Coffey for the continued review of my presentations and valuable feedback. Sean Rugless for all the free marketing advice. Bryan McCleary for the introduction to Congressman Greg Landsman. Candice Matthews Brackeen and Sean Parker for the candid feedback about my products. Pete Blackshaw for being one of my greatest cheerleaders, and the entire Cintrifuse team for their endless support. Abby Grimm for making me the "Mayor of Union Hall."

At Jungle Jim's, Kofi Hayford, Paul Fischersser, Jim Beckett, and Jimmy Bonaminio for helping me get my products into Jungle Jim's stores and grow my business with Jungle Jim's International Market.

At True Shea: Stephanie Schneider, for all the support she provided to True Shea even before she joined True Shea. Mariellen Volt and Shaquile Riston for all the support they provide me in growing my business.

In Ghana: Fati Alhassan for the support with True Shea operation in Ghana. Tony Lithur and Barima Kweku Dua for all the legal advice. Delphina Jones for being a great cheerleader.

To my cheerleaders: Ericka McGinnis for the early support and testing and recommendations for improvements to True Shea products. Mary McWhorters for being one of the greatest cheerleaders for True Shea and passing out True Shea samples everywhere she went. Digger and Chris for all the moral support. Mike Flynn for showing me around Cincinnati when I first arrived. Christoper Che for the introduction to Walmart.

At American Micro Products: Pete Kleinhenz and Jackie Ferguson for all the operations and logistical support.

Q & A FOR THE READER

I wrote this book for entrepreneurs (current and future), the immigrant community, and foreign students who want to study here and potentially start their own businesses. Entrepreneurship is not for everyone. It is a rewarding path not without its challenges, pressures, and obstacles. This path is unpredictable. If you like roller coasters—and by that I mean weathering the ups and downs and unpredictability of starting your own business—then this may be the journey for you.

Q: What is the biggest entrepreneurial myth?

A: "I want to go into business because I want to be my own boss." Please know that this business is going to boss you more than your own boss. It's with you 24/7. In an office, your boss will haunt you only eight hours a day, whereas when you are your own boss, you will haunt yourself 24/7.

Q: What do you think has made you successful?

A: Perseverance, perseverance, perseverance. Success is possible, but it's only possible because of perseverance. You have to go the extra mile and do it. What I want people to take away if they are ready to set up their own business or scale an existing business comes from Winston Churchill: "Success consists of going from failure to failure without loss of enthusiasm."

Q: I know you said not to quit your day job, but I feel ready. Do you think in my case I should quit?

A: Not so fast. How do you know you're ready? Readiness can mean lots of things.

After working full-time in corporate America for almost two decades, I turned in my resignation to work full-time at True Shea, but only after four years of building my business while holding down my full-time job. Your day job is a valuable stepping stone to allow you to get the funding to create your business while simultaneously allowing you to continue to enjoy the standard of living you currently have. Yes, there will be sacrifices and nights of lost sleep, but in the end, if you persevere, you will start to experience success just as I have.

Readiness could mean that you have five thousand dollars in the bank. Readiness could mean you have generated X amount of revenue. Revenue could mean anything. Most of the people I know who quit their job come back to corporate America in less than a year. As much as I hate to say it, it takes three to four years to really get on your feet and get going. Based on your own expenses and your own experience, do you think five thousand dollars is going to stretch that far?

That's the decision you have to make. Maybe you know how to manage money very well, and five thousand dollars will carry you for three or four years. It always takes a little longer than you think, so you have to give yourself a little bump in the race by staying employed.

You probably should do both your day job and your new job at the same time for a little longer. Some people scale down the day job without quitting so they have health benefits. Some people's spouses have jobs that provide insurance, so even if they quit, they are covered. But if you don't, maybe you should stay put so at least you have health insurance.

Q: What do you mean when you say, "Sometimes you have to go backward to go forward"?

A: For example, my original plan was to get to X amount of sales, but I didn't get there, and I wasn't getting there. I had a proven model, we had sales of around thirty thousand dollars, we had product in the store, but at first it seemed I didn't have enough to quit my day job. But it was hard to give my all to my company, because I was going between the two. To take the business to a whole new level, I had to make a sacrifice—I had to go backward in order to go forward. I had to leave my day job and focus on the business. This meant I would lose a significant portion of my income. However, sometimes you have to go backward to go forward, so that's exactly what I did.

It was just like coming from Ghana to the United States. After struggling for a long while in Ghana, I found a job with Maersk that gave me a certain level off stability for about a year, and then I came here. I had to find a job, a car, everything. I had to find a way to stop sleeping on the floor. It felt like I was starting life over again, and I questioned myself. But I had to go backward to go forward.

Q: What advice do you have for getting comfortable with networking?

A: First, you need to give yourself a good reason for doing it. You have to be convinced that going to events and networking and talking to people will help your business. If you believe that, it's half the job; it has to come from the inside. You have to feel it in your heart. Just like anything else, once you're convinced this will help you move ahead, then you find the ways and means to do it.

Take baby steps. Just start talking to people at the grocery store. Say hello to people. When you walk into a building, be nice to people. When you have a conversation with somebody, whether you're buying something or transacting business, talk a little more because those people are paid to talk to you.

You have to throw yourself out there, or somebody has to throw you out there, because that's the game changer. You'll never be able to volunteer on your own to make a big leap. So, you have to put yourself in situations where you are forcing yourself to do it or where somebody is calling on you to do it.

Q: How can I overcome my fear of speaking in front of groups?

A: Go to networking events. Have fun. Have conviction. Believe in yourself. Keep going. Be ready at a moment's notice to pitch.

Don't put too much pressure on yourself because, in the beginning, you don't even know how to network. You don't even know how to talk. Just go out there and have fun and meet people. One thing will lead to another.

Consider joining Toastmasters. True story: when I joined Toastmasters, the very first time, when it was my turn to speak, I quit. My mentor had to look for me and bring me back. I went back eventually, when I realized this was something I needed if I wanted to get to the next level.

I speak from experience when I say that it's frightening to speak in front of a big group. The most important thing, though, is conviction. If you really believe you have to do it, you will find ways to do it. When I finally got the courage to stand in front of my Toastmasters class, the first thing I said was "I never thought this day would ever happen." Everybody started cracking up—especially me.

I had to practice—a lot. I practiced in front of my daughter. I practiced in front of my wife at the time. I knew I had to do this, because eventually I would need to pitch my ideas to other companies and investors.

Q: How do you hook someone's interest? How do you keep them listening?

A: Early on, I hooked my first major investor and mentor, and he's been my mentor for the last eighteen years. This is how I did it. When I go to a networking event or speaking engagement, I look at all the speakers who are going to speak that day. I look at five or six of the speakers and think, *Okay, out of all these speakers, who do I need the most?* Then I decide on the most important question I can ask that person. You don't have a lot of time, so you have to make it count.

How do you press that trigger point to get them interested? Right after the event, you go and follow up and have a good conversation. But you have to do your homework beforehand so you have an idea of what this person's trigger point is. Everybody has a trigger point. You want to use that to make some kind of connection, either something you share in common or something they are really passionate about.

This is why I have so many mentors. I have around one hundred of them. Take Steve Hightower. I knew he was in the petroleum business, and Ghana had just discovered oil and petroleum. So I asked him something about the petroleum industry, and I let him know that Ghana had a lot of petroleum products. I asked him what he thought about the petroleum products industry in general. Letting him know that Ghana has petroleum as well made sure he was immediately interested in my question. I made a connection with him right away because I did my homework. Petroleum was his trigger point.

You need to get comfortable approaching people you don't know, and you need to do your homework to create that connection. Sometimes it happens naturally, but sometimes you have to make it happen. And then there are times when you meet someone by surprise, like when I met Carl at Kroger doing his shopping. When opportunities like that happen, you can't freeze. You have to be ready to approach people.

Q: How many different kinds of pitches do you need?

A: You need a short one: the elevator pitch. That's the one for quick interactions, when you need to catch someone's attention in a few seconds. When you have the whole room to yourself and the audience is there to listen, you want to have a more elaborate strategy. And then you need the in-between pitches, when you have fifteen or thirty minutes—not a lot of time. That requires a different approach.

The key to all these pitches is your opening, because if you don't get people's attention within the first thirty or sixty seconds, it becomes more difficult. Even if it's a three-hour pitch, in the first minute, you have to hook them in immediately.

Q: You are very generous. You give back to others. What made you want to give to others?

A: I know what it is to struggle. I don't want others to struggle like I did. I try to give back to help others.

Q: When did you first know you were an entrepreneur?

A: My father was an entrepreneur. I learned from him, and I liked it. When I was fifteen or sixteen, right after I lost my mother, I was thrown into survival mode. I needed to make money for myself immediately. In Ghana, the easiest job is the job you create for yourself. It's not like you can go work at McDonald's. I have an entrepreneurial spirit like my father. That's why I packed my suitcases and flew to America.

Q: What was your first product?

A: My first product wasn't necessarily one particular product. I became a general merchandiser. Back then, there wasn't any YouTube or Amazon. So I looked around for opportunity. For example, let's say I know you, and you have ten shoes. I'll ask whether you want to sell any of your old shoes. If you say yes, I'll say, "How much do you want for the shoes?" You say you want ten bucks. I say okay, and I go out in the market, which is my neighborhood, and say, "Hey, who wants to buy some shoes?" Then another guy says, "Well, I want a pair of shoes, but I don't have any money. But I do have a shirt." I'd say okay, and we'd swap products. I match them up, I sell it, I take a little cut from each person, and start doing business like that.

I grew into selling about eighty different things. At one point, in my community, I became known as the guy who could sell this and that. When my friends went to parties or nightclubs, most of them were there to drink and have fun. That wasn't me, and I usually went out to parties or gatherings without a date as this was my hustling time For me, that was the moment I would close my deals. I went to parties because I had become a broker in the community, and parties were prime time for me. I was just connecting with people and taking cash. At some point, I became the broker for the town.

When I went to school, I talked to my parents' friends or my sister's friends, and I'd ask, "Hey, you got shoes?" They'd say, "Yeah, I got shoes." I'd say, "Okay, why don't you give me fifteen or twenty dollars' worth of your shoes. I'm going to go to college. I'll go sell your shoes for you. When I sell them, I'll bring you the money for your products." So I was moving product in my dorm room at college—ladies' shoes, chocolate, paper, things like that.

My room was like a department store, full of all kinds of things. I was moving products and still managing to get good grades. That's how it all started. When I came to the United States, I guess I did the same thing. I thought, *Okay, now I have an MBA. Now that I have worked in corporate America, let me go and talk to people in corporate America.* I talked to Cintas Corporation. I encouraged the CEO of Cintas to introduce me to the sourcing team to source uniforms from Ghana. Then I went and talked to the people in Ghana for him.

I met with the vice president of Ghana, His Excellency John Dramani Mahama. I told him, "Hey, I have this deal. I can supply uniforms to Cintas." I brought the two of them together, and we closed the deal. So, I just elevated what I used to do growing up as the area broker in my community. I took it to a different level once I had my MBA. But the fundamentals are still the same today as back then.

That's my strength: bringing people together. I don't have any money to do it, but I can convince people that with hard work, determination, and strategy, it can happen. It's in my blood. Being a broker back when I was a teenager taught me how to build relationships. I learned the value of people and the value of relationships.

Q: When you say people undervalue relationships, what do you mean?

A: If someone likes you, they are more likely to listen to you and more likely to work with you. Cultivate a solid relationship; the polish comes later. Make it a warm relationship in order for the person to like you and listen to you. Data is important. But before you get to data, the relationship comes first.

Q: What advice do you have for a new entrepreneur?

A: You must love your work. Not only must you love your work, you must be obsessed with your work. You must live it, breathe it, dream it. It's always on your mind, even when you're asleep. If you're not having nightmares about your product, you're doing something wrong.

Sometimes, those nightmares can help you prepare before something actually becomes a problem. They can help you solve something before it turns into a disaster. Sometimes, if you need an answer to a problem, you might get it in your dreams.

You have to believe in your product and yourself and the journey. You have to trust the journey and have faith. It's a leap of faith.

Q: How important is it to believe in your product?

A: It's very important to believe in your product, yourself, and your journey. You are your biggest cheerleader. The other supporting cheerleaders will come and go; some will stay, some will leave, some will come back, et cetera. Everything revolves around you. Others will feed off the vibes from you. You must not only be passionate about your product; you must be obsessed with it.

I pitched a business deal in Ghana many, many years ago to the country's senior presidential advisor. I told her I wanted to bring an operation to Ghana and run it, but I didn't want to go to Ghana. I wanted to outsource it in Ghana and let them produce it. She said, "Manny, I just met with you for thirty minutes. The passion you are bringing to the game is huge. I mean, I can feel it hitting me." The vibe has to come from you. If you don't believe in it, that vibe is not going to show, and nobody's going to follow you.

Q: Are you planning to create more products under the True Shea umbrella?

A: We just rolled out lotion and foot balm. And we have some other things in the pipeline.

Q: How can you make your disadvantage an advantage?

A: When I attended Xavier University, at one point I was struggling; I was feeling bad. A friend in New York said, "Imagine you are in prison for two years. There is an exact end date. Just do your best for two years." That helped me to see a light at the end of the tunnel. Put everything you have in the two years in prison, and it will pay off when you are released.

Q: When raising money for your company, should you go into debt or go for equity?

A: My answer is a combination of both, depending on your strengths and weaknesses. Debt is a loan, which you will have to pay back at one point with monthly interest rates. If you go into too much debt, your monthly interest rate might be high, and it might affect the cash flow of your business. It might not leave you with too much money.

Secondly, in order to get a loan, you need to have a good credit score. It's good to have a job. If you don't have those things, you may not be able to get much of a loan. So your only option might be equity.

Some debt is okay, like when I started with my credit cards. I kept my day job, but I had credit cards and would put what I needed on the credit cards and then pay them off. Eventually I would get a credit card with a bigger credit limit, and so forth. If you have a job and your credit score is good, you can get 0 percent interest rates. You won't get that if you don't have a job or a good credit score. They go hand in hand.

Q: What do you mean by *equity*?
A: Equity is getting investors to invest their money in your company. Equity investors buy shares in your company. They stay with you and participate in the ups and downs of your company.

Q: How much of my company should I "give away"?
A: One hundred percent of zero is zero. Some profit is better than no profit. There is no need to hold on to everything. Don't be greedy. Some people want to hold on to all their shares in their company. My point is if you own everything and you have a zero company valuation, 100 percent of that is zero.

Q: Should I produce in-house or outsource production?
A: It depends on your strengths and how you want to proceed. For in-house production, you need a loan, equipment, et cetera. If you can't pay back the loan, the banks will come after you and your business. There's a high profit margin but also a high risk. If you outsource,

there's low risk. You're not investing in equipment. It's done for you. But there's less margin. There's a trade-off for that lower risk. In the beginning, I recommend starting in-house. When your business grows, then you can outsource.

The trade-off is not just money. It's also risk. It's also time involved, energy, and resources. I don't want to be living in my basement full-time making shea butter. I'm happy to outsource my product. That way, I can focus on growing my business. If I tried to do everything, my business wouldn't grow.

So, like me, you may start in-house, but as your business grows, you outsource once you grow and can meet the outsourcing requirements for high-volume jobs. For example, if you need someone to make ten or fifteen T-shirts, you're probably not ready for outsourcing. But if you need ten thousand T-shirts, that is a different situation.

Finding that sweet spot where demand exceeds supply is different for different people. I knew I had to leave the basement operation once Kroger came along, because I would be going from five stores to three hundred stores. Someone might look at their business and say, "If I get to ten thousand dollars in revenue a month or fifty thousand dollars in revenue a month, I'll have to produce X amount of units." That person knows that once they hit ten thousand units, they have to start moving outside, because that's all they have. So, it's different for different people, but you have to figure it out for yourself.

Q: How do I prepare for surprises in my business?

A: Running a business is like being a president of a country. No amount of preparation can prepare you for emergencies, surprises, et cetera. But you need to have certain skills and a foundation to be able to withstand the surprises. You must be flexible. Life will always throw you curveballs. Be ready to work extra hours. Be ready to act fast.

Q: Talk to me more about the Africa Water Project.

A: I plan on expanding my business to source products from other African countries and sell those products in the U.S. The model is to donate a water well in whichever African country the product is sourced from. Africa Water Project is bigger than just water. We are also providing economic opportunities for the people in Ghana, where we source some of the shea butter. And with the proceeds from our sales, we're creating economic opportunity for clean drinking water and jobs. Drinking water is an Africa problem; it's not just a Ghana problem. So I see this expanding to all of Africa one day—to be able to provide clean drinking water and economic growth for the entire continent.

Whatever the product is, we'll import it from Africa. So we'll bring cashews from the Côte d'Ivoire to Cincinnati to process them. This will be a raw product, just like shea butter. That way, we create employment opportunities in both Africa and Cincinnati. And then we'll sell it to the Walmarts and the Targets, and then take the money back and build more wells in Africa from the proceeds of these sales.

This is the same model we are using for shea butter. Today, when we bring shea butter from Ghana into the United States, we create jobs in Ghana because we mix shea butter there. When we produce it in Cincinnati, we create paying jobs here. Then we take it to Kroger, and we use those proceeds to build a water well in Ghana.

The plan is that from whatever country we source the raw material, at the end of the day, the well goes to the country that provided the raw product. If we bring the products from Côte d'Ivoire and sell it to the United States, we build the well in Côte d'Ivoire. If we bring the product from Nigeria and sell it in the United States, then the well goes to Nigeria. So where the business is sourced, the well goes back there.

Q: Community is important to you. Do you think that is part of your culture and also comes from being part of a large family?

A: Without a doubt, it's a communal thing. Friends, family, my mother's friends, just people, community—Africa is a communal society. Because it's a communal society, you want to share what you have; you want to share your culture. In the United States, if you go out, everyone splits the tab. You pay for your own meal. In Africa, if you have friends, one person picks up the tab; you just take turns. The next time, someone else picks up the tab. Sharing and giving are part of that communal experience.

Q: I have done all I know how to do, but I am stuck.

A: Owning your own business is a challenging journey. Know that your skills—all the things you know how to do—are just the beginning. You need to learn everything you don't know how to do in order to be successful. At this point you need to reach beyond your current network to include mentors and community resources, including your chamber of commerce and other organizations. This is when you need to think outside the box.

ABOUT THE AUTHOR

Manny Addo is the CEO of Cincinnati-based Natural Shea Care (NSC). NSC is a Black-owned natural beauty care company with a mission of supporting and empowering the women of Ghana, where the shea butter for its products is sourced. Currently, NSC has distributed products in more than five thousand stores in the United States and Canada in the last five years, and products are available across the United States, including Kroger, Jungle Jim's International Market, Target.com, Amazon, TJ Maxx, and Marshalls. Manny's educational, cultural, and professional exposure in Africa and the United States enables him to successfully promote business between these regions.

Manny is also the CEO of Africa America Business Promotion, a company that promotes business between Africa and the United States. In this capacity, he organized the first Africa America Trade and Investment Summit at the Cincinnati Chamber of Commerce in July

2018. This event was attended by Ghana's minister of trade, Ghana's ambassador to the United States, the president of Cintas Corporation, and representatives from Kroger, Procter & Gamble, and businesses from Canada, China, and New York.

Manny has an MBA in finance and marketing from Xavier University and a bachelor's degree in social science and a diploma in education from the University of Cape Coast. He worked as a senior financial analyst for General Electric, Fifth Third Bank, Duke Energy, PricewaterhouseCoopers, and JPMorgan Chase. He also worked with Maersk Sealand as an export officer, giving him experience in customs clearance and supply chain management. Manny is a member of the Cincinnati Chamber of Commerce, the Ohio Minority Supply Development Council, and the Cincinnati African American Chamber of Commerce.

Manny was nominated by Kroger and went on to win the Ohio Minority Supply Development Council (OMSDC) Class 1 award in 2020, and he won the OMSDC award for Emerging Business of the Year in 2022.

In 2023, Manny met with Congressman Greg Landsman, U.S. representative for Ohio's first congressional district, and asked him to recommend him for President Joe Biden's Advisory Council on African Diaspora Engagement, which he did. Although he was not selected, he received a letter from President Biden to thank him and encourage him to apply for other jobs in his administration.

Manny resides in Cincinnati, Ohio. This is his first book. To learn more about Manny and True Shea, visit www.naturalsheacare.com.